A Road Map for

Facilitating
Collaborative Teams

Peggy Hayden
Linda Frederick
Barbara J. Smith

3M™ Spray Mount™ is a trademark of 3M.

ISBN 1-57035-800-1

Edited by Sandra L. Knauke
Text layout and design by Eileen Bechtold
Cover design by Eileen Bechtold

09 08 07 06   6 5 4 3 2

Printed in the United States of America
Published and Distributed by

Sopris West™
EDUCATIONAL SERVICES

A Cambium Learning Company

4093 Specialty Place • Longmont, Colorado 80504
(303) 651-2829 • www.sopriswest.com

IDEAs
that
Work
Office of Special
Education Programs

This manuscript was prepared in part with support from the U.S. Office of
Special Education Programs, grant # H324R980047-99 to the University of
Colorado at Denver. The opinions are not necessarily those of the U.S. Office
of Special Education Programs or the University of Colorado at Denver.

29671/205ROAD/09-06

Acknowledgments

This manual provides reasons and resources for creating collaborative teams to promote meaningful change in local early childhood systems. It was developed based on research on effective practice related to systems change and teaming/collaboration and the experiences of the Collaborative Planning Project (CPP) for Comprehensive Early Childhood Systems. CPP was a three-year (1998–2001) federal outreach project funded with support from the U.S. Office of Special Education Programs and based at the Center for Collaborative Educational Leadership, University of Colorado at Denver. The project provided training and technical assistance (TA) to local interagency teams to:

1. Create a coordinated system of early care and education services to young children birth through five (or up to age eight) and their families;

2. Improve relationships and communication among the agencies that compose the system;

3. Maximize and blend resources; and

4. Improve the likelihood that *all* children can have positive child outcomes as a result of family-friendly services in quality, inclusive settings.

In addition to this replication manual, the project produced the following papers:

- Hayden, P., Frederick, L., Smith, B. J., & Broudy, A. (2001a). *Developmental facilitation: Helping teams promote systems change*. Denver: Collaborative Planning Project for Planning Comprehensive Early Childhood Systems at the University of Colorado at Denver. ERIC #ED455628

- Hayden, P., Frederick, L., Smith, B. J., & Broudy, A. (2001b). *Tasks, tips, and tools for promoting collaborative community teams*. Denver: Collaborative Planning Project for Planning Comprehensive Early Childhood Systems at the University of Colorado at Denver. ERIC #ED455627

- Hayden, P., Smith, B. J., Rapport, M. J., & Frederick, L. (1999). *Facilitating change in comprehensive early childhood systems.* Denver: Collaborative Planning Project for Planning Comprehensive Early Childhood Systems at the University of Colorado at Denver. ERIC #ED435152

- Smith, B. J., & Rapport, M. J. (1999a). *Early childhood inclusion policy and systems: What do we know?* Denver: Collaborative Planning Project for Planning Comprehensive Early Childhood Systems at the University of Colorado at Denver. ERIC #ED436035

- Smith, B. J., & Rapport, M. J. (1999b). *IDEA and early childhood inclusion.* Denver: Collaborative Planning Project for Planning Comprehensive Early Childhood Systems at the University of Colorado at Denver. ERIC #ED436036

The authors of this manual would like to acknowledge the contributions of the following state and local collaborative teams and individuals. Their input provided valuable direction for the development of the concepts and resources contained in this manual.

State Level Collaborative Teams

- Rhode Island Early Childhood Interagency Task Force

- West Virginia Early Childhood Transition Steering Committee

Local Community Collaborative Planning Project (CPP) Teams

- Acadia Parish, Crowley, LA, CPP Team

- Cranston, RI, CPP Team

- Central Falls, RI, CPP Team

- Denver, CO, CPP Team

- Greater Metropolitan Clark County, Las Vegas, NV, CPP Team

- St. Vrain Early Childhood Council, Longmont, CO, CPP Team

- South Kingstown, RI, CPP Team

- Westerly, RI, CPP Team

Field Reviewers

- Linda Askew

- Jennifer DeFrance

- Ellie Valdez Honeyman

- Tracey Maron

About the Authors

Peggy Hayden is a consultant to state and local education and human services agencies. She has been a special education teacher, a state level administrator, and a regional early intervention (birth to 5) agency director. She has been the principal investigator and consultant to federally funded demonstration and outreach projects including projects related to interagency collaboration among education, Head Start, early intervention, and other agencies. She has chaired several state and local interagency advisory groups. She has provided keynotes, awareness, and in-depth training at national, state, and local levels on early childhood transition; group facilitation and training strategies; interagency collaboration; legal requirements for children with disabilities and their families; organizational development; passing state legislation; working with advisory groups and boards; teacher assistants; and win-win conflict resolution. Honors include KY Division for Early Childhood Contributor of the Year, 1990; KY Council for Exceptional Children (CEC) Member of the Year, 1986; KY CEC Special Education Administrator of the Year, 1983; and Special Education Teacher of the Year, KY Association for Retarded Citizens, 1972. Degrees include a B.A. (summa cum laude), an M.A. in Special Education, and a Rank I (M.A. plus 30 hours) in Education Administration/certification as Director of Special Education.

Linda Frederick is the parent of two sons, the youngest of whom was born with Down syndrome in 1982. Since then, Linda has worked extensively with collaborative systems change teams at local, state, and national levels. Her experiences include parent-to-parent support, advocacy for people with disabilities, and as a teacher and trainer in the fields of health care, case management, inclusive education, and legislation. Organizations she has worked with include the Mile High Down Syndrome Association, Coloradans for Family Support, Governor's Council on Restructuring State Government, the Denver Chamber of Commerce Leadership Denver, and the Division for Early Childhood's board of directors. Linda has worked as a professional research assistant with national early childhood efforts at the *University of Colorado Health Science Center: Western Region Faculty Institute for Training,* the *University of Colorado at Denver: Collaborative Planning Project for Comprehensive Early Childhood Systems,* and the *Division for Early Childhood's Recommended Practices Bridging the Gap* project. Her degree is a B.A. in Russian Area Studies, Liberal Arts from Colorado College.

Barbara J. Smith is an Associate Research Professor in The School of Education at the University of Colorado at Denver. She was the Executive Director of the Division for Early Childhood, Council for Exceptional Children for 12 years. Dr. Smith is a recognized expert in policy and administration issues in EI/ECSE and coordinated DEC's work in the mid-1980's that resulted in the Infant and Toddler and Preschool programs of IDEA. She has provided training and TA to professionals and families in nearly every state and in Canada, Australia, and India. She has helped develop early childhood policies and systems change efforts in Pennsylvania, Alaska, New Mexico, Maryland, and Colorado. She was the developer of an EI/ESCE systems change model, which was the foundation of this collaboration team model. She has over 50 publications related to young children with special needs including *The Administrator's Policy Handbook for Preschool Mainstreaming* and *DEC's Recommended Practices in Early Intervention/Early Childhood Special Education*. Dr. Smith has more than twenty-five years experience in the field as a teacher, researcher, teacher trainer, program developer, administrator, and policy analyst and has administered numerous public and private grants and contracts and projects of national significance.

Contents

Team Activities and Forms ix

Foreword xi

Chapter I—The Road Ahead 1
Introducing the Collaborative Planning Project (CPP)
Use of This Manual 1
Overview of CPP Project and Local CPP Teams 3
CPP Model 4

Chapter II—The Tour Guide 7
Facilitator Selection and Role
Team Stages and Behavior 9
Individual Team Member Impact (C-BAM) 9
Facilitator Role and Tasks 9

Chapter III—Getting Started 11
*Establishing Shared Leadership Commitment and
a Team Structure for Collaboration*
Getting Shared Leadership Commitment and Recruiting
Collaborative Team Participants 12
Conducting the Organizational Meeting to Get Acquainted,
Assess the Current Community Context, and Determine
the Team's Initial Focus 16
Creating an Effective Structure for the Team's Operation
Including Team Ground Rules 21
Are We There Yet? 29

Chapter IV—Fellow Travelers for the Journey 31
*Developing Meaningful Stakeholder Relationships and
Involvement*
Fostering Team Member Commitment 32
Fully Engaging a Variety of Stakeholders 33
Developing Strong Teams Built on Effective
People-to-People Relationships 37
Are We There Yet? 42

Chapter V—Determining the Destination .43
Establishing a Shared Vision
Developing a Shared Team Vision Meaningful to
All Team Members 44
Extending the Vision Beyond the Team to Key Community
Stakeholders and Keeping It Alive Over Time 47
Are We There Yet? 50

Chapter VI—Mapping the Journey **51**
    Setting Priorities and Action Planning
    Setting Priorities 52
    Action Planning 58
    Are We There Yet? 71

Chapter VII—Being on the Road **73**
    Implementing Plans, Allocating Resources, and Evaluating
    Accomplishments and Teamwork
    Implementing Action Plans 74
    Allocating Resources 83
    Monitoring and Evaluating Team Accomplishments
    and Teamwork 86
    Are We There Yet? 93

Chapter VIII—Checking the Rearview Mirror **95**
    Lessons Learned
    Helping Teams Transition From One Facilitator to Another 95
    CPP Top Ten Rules of the Road for the Journey Toward
    Systems Change 96
    Concluding Remarks 99

Chapter IX—Looking Through Our Scrapbook **101**
    Profiles and Products From CPP Teams
    Crowley, LA, Acadia Parish Team Profile 101
    Central Falls, RI, CPP Team Profile .104
    Cranston, RI, CPP Team Profile 114
    Denver, CO, CPP Team Profile 132
    Las Vegas, NV, Greater Metropolitan Clark County
    CPP Team Profile 143
    South Kingstown, RI, CPP Team Profile 146
    Longmont, CO, St. Vrain Early Childhood Council
    CPP Team Profile 155
    Westerly, RI, CPP Team Profile 158

Bibliography **165**

Team Activities and Forms

Sample Letter Asking Potential Team Members to Attend the
Organizational Meeting 14

RSVP Regarding Attending Collaborative Team Meeting 15

Collaborative Team Organizational Meeting Agenda 17

Activity—Assessing Your Community's Strengths, Weaknesses,
Opportunities, and Threats (SWOTs) 20

Activity—Activity to Determine a Team's Initial Focus 21

Collaborative Planning Team Minutes Shell 23

Sample Ground Rules for the Team to Adapt as Appropriate 26

Collaborative Planning Team Input Form .36

Activity—Building a Team Resume 38

Agency Profile 40

Activity—Visioning Activity 46

Activity—Activity to Identify Priority Challenges the Team
Will Address Via Action Planning 53

Collaborative Planning Team Action Plan Form 60

Instructions for Collaborative Planning Team Action Plan Form . . .61

Activity—Action Planning Activity 62

Activity—Round Robin Activity for Editing Multiple
Action Plans 69

Generic Format for an Interagency Collaboration Agreement 77

Sample Press Release 81

Sample Evaluation Plan 89

Facilitating Collaborative Teams

Foreword

Background: This manual provides reasons and resources for creating collaborative teams to promote meaningful change in local early childhood systems. It was developed based on research on effective practice related to systems change, teaming/collaboration, and the experiences of the Collaborative Planning Project (CPP) for Comprehensive Early Childhood Systems. CPP was a three-year (1998–2001) federal outreach project funded through the Individuals with Disabilities Education Act and based at the Center for Collaborative Educational Leadership, University of Colorado-Denver. The project provided training and technical assistance (TA) to eight local interagency/CPP teams across four states to support them in:

1. Creating a coordinated system of early care and education services to young children birth through five (or up to age eight) and their families;

2. Improving relationships and communication among the agencies that compose the system;

3. Maximizing and blending resources; and

4. Improving the likelihood that ALL children can have positive child outcomes as a result of family-friendly services in quality, inclusive settings.

Intended Audience: State administrative and TA staff; local administrators, local Interagency Coordinating Councils (ICCs), and other local collaborative teams.

Manual Overview: Chapters I and II introduce the manual. Chapters III–VII provide step-by-step guidance and resources for implementing the CPP model. These chapters are organized in a question (*Which way to go?*) and answer (*Directions*) format. The following resource information is embedded throughout each chapter: *Backseat Driving*—Facilitation and collaboration tips; *Souvenirs*—Reflections and examples from local CPP teams; *Activities*—Specific instructions for carrying out various team tasks; and *Forms*—Samples that teams can use or adapt. Chapters III–VII each end with a section called

"Are We There Yet? Advice on helping teams evaluate their progress and evolve to the next stage." Chapter VIII provides CPP staff reflections and concluding remarks. Finally, Chapter IX provides detailed CPP team profiles that tell the team's "story," including accomplishments, reflections, and team products (e.g., plans and forms). Profiles were completed three to six months after CPP staff finished working with the team and then later updated through a follow-up that is included at the end of each profile in the section, "Where Are They Now (Winter 2001–02)?"

Analytical Table of Contents

Chapter I—The Road Ahead: Introducing the Collaborative Planning Project (CPP)

1. Use of This Manual

2. Overview of CPP Project and Local CPP Teams

3. CPP Model

Chapter II—The Tour Guide: Facilitator Selection and Role

1. Team Stages and Behavior

2. Individual Team Member Impact (C-BAM)

3. Facilitator Role and Tasks

Chapter III—Getting Started: Establishing Shared Leadership Commitment and a Team Structure for Collaboration

1. Getting Shared Leadership Commitment and Recruiting Collaborative Team Participants

- Which agencies should be invited to be involved on the collaborative team?

- How can shared leadership commitment from these agencies be ensured?

- Which staff from these agencies need to be involved on the team?

- How can the interests of families be effectively represented on the team?

- What steps need to be taken to invite potential team members to an organizational meeting?

- What do you do if one or more of the agencies you think need to be on the team refuses to participate?

2. Conducting the Organizational Meeting to Get Acquainted, Assess the Current Community Context, and Determine the Team's Initial Focus

- Who will facilitate and take minutes at the first meeting?

- Where will the meeting be held?

- What are key issues that need to be addressed at the organizational meeting? How much time should be allocated?

- What are strategies for helping team members develop a common understanding of the services provided by the agencies represented on the team?

- What are strategies for helping team members evaluate current early childhood services in the community as a preliminary step to deciding the focus that the team wants to take?

- How does the team decide on a focus or basic direction to which all members are willing to commit and devote time and effort?

3. Creating an Effective Structure for the Team's Operation Including Team Ground Rules

- Who will be the core team members? What agencies will be involved on an ad hoc basis?

- What are key roles on the team that need to be filled to ensure that as many team members as possible are actively involved in the team's operation?

- What is an effective and easy-to-use format for meeting minutes? What are recommended timelines and distribution strategies for minutes?

- What authority does the team have? Can the team make decisions independent of the agencies represented on the team? What will be done if the team cannot agree?

- When and where will team meetings regularly take place? What are guidelines for effective meeting operation?

- What will the team do about absentees?

- How will the team handle interpersonal dynamics in meetings? What supports will be in place for building positive team relationships?

- How will the team members communicate with others in their respective agencies, including their respective agency chains of command, line staff, and families? What strategies will be used to ensure ongoing information exchange both to share information and to solicit input from a variety of stakeholders? How will the team communicate with other key agencies/stakeholders in the community that are not represented on the team?

- How will the team orient new team members so that they feel welcomed on the team and can be effective contributors?

4. Are We There Yet?

Chapter IV—Fellow Travelers for the Journey: Developing Meaningful Stakeholder Relationships and Involvement

1. Fostering Team Member Commitment

- Has the team's intention to collaborate come about because of external factors? Have they been told by someone else that they must collaborate (e.g., a state or federal mandate)? Do federal and state legal requirements, grants, or other resources influence collaborative efforts?

- Has this intention to collaborate come about because of internal factors based on local community needs? Is this one person/agency's idea or does there seem to be general agreement on the need to collaborate? What needs do individual team members and their constituencies have for which collaboration is a means to an end rather than an end in itself? Why would people find it beneficial to spend already limited time working together? How can

the facilitator help team members move from being mentally tuned into the "radio station" WIIFM (What's In It For Me) into WIIFMC (What's In It For My Community)?

- Is a motivating factor a "threat" (e.g., the closing of a local program that will create a big service gap) or an "opportunity" (e.g., the chance to apply for a collaborative grant) for which people may feel a greater sense of urgency to collaborate? Can the team turn a threat into an opportunity for collaboration and systems change?

2. Fully Engaging a Variety of Stakeholders

- Who should be on the team?

- How can teams ensure that their size is manageable and yet be responsive to a variety of stakeholders?

- What is the chain of command within the agencies represented on the team that the team will need to consider in order to get respective agencies' approval for team plans? What is each team member's role in relation to the chain of command of his or her agency? Is he or she a decision-maker? Does he or she have ready access to decision-makers, e.g., serving as the decision-makers designee on the team? Are team members administrative staff with some authority over people who may ultimately be asked to implement collaborative team plans? Are they a peer of people who may ultimately implement collaborative team plans? Are there already established channels within the respective agencies that the team can access for information sharing and gathering input of agency staff that will ultimately serve in an approval or implementer role?

- For team members that are parents, are they on the team representing a parent perspective on their own or do they represent a group of parents?

- Who are others in the community whose input or buy-in the team needs but who should not or cannot be regular members of the core team? Do any core team members have effective working relation-ships with these people?

3. Developing Strong Teams Built on Effective People-to-People Relationships

- How can team members get to know each other as individuals?

- How can team members get to know each other as agencies?

- Do team members have a positive history of working together individually or collective-ly? If positive, how can this history be relat-ed to this new collaboration?

- Do team members have a negative history of working together individually or collec-tively? Who were the involved parties? What happened? What evidence exists, if any, that a negative impact is still being felt? That is, is it in the past or is this past still affecting the way that people interact with each other? How is this manifesting itself? What were the root causes of this negativity and how can they be addressed in a way to create a more positive climate for collaboration?

- What are strategies for promoting harmo-nious team interactions?

- What are tools for conflict resolution?

4. Are We There Yet?

Chapter V—Determining the Destination: Establishing a Shared Vision

1. Developing a Shared Team Vision Meaningful to All Team Members

- How can the team ensure that the vision is "real" for team members? What strategies help team members buy into the vision and actively work toward its achievement? How can the team ensure that the vision meets both individual agency and community needs?

- What if team members have trouble think-ing beyond the day-to-day and thus consider it meaningless to think about the future? What if they see their problems as beyond

their control? What if they are preoccupied with doing only that which they are required legally to do?

- What is an activity that will fully involve all team members in vision formulation?

2. Extending the Vision Beyond the Team to Key Community Stakeholders and Keeping It Alive Over Time

- Can you change the vision?

- How can the team build support for the vision in the community beyond core team members?

- How do you keep the vision alive over time?

3. Are We There Yet?

Chapter VI—Mapping the Journey: Setting Priorities and Action Planning

1. Setting Priorities

- What criteria will the team use for priority setting?

- What are priority challenges that reflect gaps between the community's current context and the vision the team would like to create? How can these be identified in a way that seems fair to all? What if team members have trouble agreeing on priorities?

- Which challenges should the team tackle first? How many challenges should the team try to address in its initial activities?

- Does the team have enough information on which to base decisions about priority set-ting or to move from priority setting to Action Planning?

2. Action Planning

- What are the action plan components through which the team addresses the iden-tified challenges? What are strategies the team can use for action plan development?

- Should the team confine Action Planning to the core team or involve other stakeholders?

- Do the agencies and individuals identified as having some role in plan implementation have the capacity to carry out those roles?

3. Are We There Yet?

Chapter VII—Being on the Road: Implementing Plans, Allocating Resources, and Evaluating Accomplishments and Teamwork

1. Implementing Action Plans

- How can the team support agencies and people in making the changes required in the plans? What are strategies for building motivation and intervening positively with resistance?

- How can the team effectively manage and coordinate plan implementation? What happens to the action plans once they are written? What is their relevance to team meetings after they are written?

- How can the team track and document plan implementation and team decisions?

- How can the team keep key stakeholders informed about plan implementation? What are strategies for communicating plan implementation information and decisions within the team, among those impacted by plan implementation and with the community at large?

- How can teams deal with "implementation dips" and keep people motivated?

2. Allocating Resources

- What is meant by the term "resources?" Is this only money or does it mean other types of resources as well?

- What will collaborative plans cost? Will collaboration require a grant or new funding? What if community agencies do not have "extra" resources to commit to collaboration?

- How can a community offer new services without new money? How can collaborative services be financed?

- Are there funds for which teams can apply on a collaborative basis? Who serves as the fiscal agent? Does the team need to be incorporated?

3. Monitoring and Evaluating Team Accomplishments and Teamwork

- How can the team ensure that plans are being implemented as planned? What if some element on the plan does not seem to be working? What if new issues emerge that the team had not anticipated—both those that relate to the plan and those that might get the team off track?

- Is the plan producing the desired results? Are the identified challenges being addressed in a way that takes the team toward its vision? Is the team operating effectively? Is membership still appropriate? Are all team members doing their part?

- When the team completes implementation of its plan, what then?

4. Are We There Yet?

Chapter VIII—Checking the Rearview Mirror: Lessons Learned

1. Helping Teams Transition From One Facilitator to Another

2. CPP Top Ten Rules of the Road for the Journey Toward Systems Change

3. Concluding Remarks

Chapter IX—Looking Through Our Scrapbook: Profiles and Products From CPP Teams

1. Crowley, LA, Acadia Parish Team Profile

2. Central Falls, RI, CPP Team Profile

3. Cranston, RI, CPP Team Profile

4. Denver, CO, CPP Team Profile

5. Las Vegas, NV, Greater Metropolitan Clark County CPP Team Profile

6. South Kingstown, RI, CPP Team Profile

7. Longmont, CO, St. Vrain Early Childhood Council CPP Team Profile

8. Westerly, RI, CPP Team Profile

Chapter I

The Road Ahead

Introducing the Collaborative Planning Project (CPP)

This chapter:

- Addresses the use of this manual;

- Provides an overview of the CPP project and local CPP teams; and

- Explains the CPP model.

Use of This Manual

A major learning of Collaborative Planning Project (CPP) staff was that **effective interagency collaboration is a process, *not* a single event**. It evolves over time as a result of people spending time together, building positive working relationships, and producing outcomes that meet the individual and collective needs of team members as well as the community at large. In many respects, collaboration is a journey. That is, a group of travelers (the team) decides to travel together (collaborate) to a mutually determined destination (vision and goals/objectives). They develop an itinerary (plan) to get them to their destination. Someone serves as the tour guide (the facilitator of the journey) to make sure that the travelers successfully reach their destination. As they travel, they follow rules of the road (ground rules for effective operation). Celebrating accomplishments along the way becomes fuel to keep going. The travelers evaluate "Are we there yet?" throughout their trip as part of routine maintenance and for an evaluation of the overall journey at its conclusion. This manual uses the journey analogy as its framework.

The manual is organized as follows. Chapter I introduces the CPP model. Chapter II discusses the role of the facilitator for the group. Chapters III-VII provide step-by-step guidance and resources for implementing the CPP model. These chapters are organized in a question and answer format. The following resource information is embedded throughout each chapter:

- Backseat Driving—Facilitation and collaboration tips;

- Souvenirs—Reflections and examples from local CPP teams;

- Activities—Specific instructions for carrying out various team tasks; and

- Forms—Samples that teams can use or adapt.

Chapters III–VII each end with a section called "Are we there yet? Advice on helping teams evaluate their progress and evolve to the next stage." Chapter VIII provides CPP staff reflections and concluding remarks. Finally, Chapter IX provides detailed CPP team profiles that tell each team's "story," including accomplishments, reflections, and team products (e.g., plans and forms). Profiles were completed three to six months after CPP staff finished working with the team and then later updated through a follow-up that is included at the end of each profile in the section "Where Are They Now (Winter 2001–02)?"

This manual was developed for the following audiences.

Audience	Possible Uses
State administrative and technical assistance (TA) staff	Use the manual as a guide for TA to local teams. Have TA providers facilitate multiple sessions with each team to accomplish the key tasks outlined in the manual until the team is self-sustaining. A team is self-sustaining when it has organized as a team, accomplished at least one concrete task, and has a plan for further collaborations. The team should have completed the activities in Chapters III, IV, V, and to some degree, in Chapters VI and VII. This can generally be accomplished in five or six sessions. Use the manual to train team facilitators. It is advisable to set up some form of ongoing networking for facilitators so that they can share ideas and support each other. Networking strategies can include meetings, e-mail, and/or phone calls. Use the manual to train local teams, completing some of the activities in Chapters III, IV, V, and VI while at the training and using the remainder of the manual for follow-up after the training. Approximately three to six months following the training, communicate with teams to (1) provide encouragement for their efforts, (2) check on their progress, (3) seek feedback on training impact, and (4) ascertain support they may need. Networking strategies among teams should be pursued, e.g., e-mail, newsletters, conference calls, and periodic meetings. Disseminate the manual to local teams for use as a guide for facilitating local efforts. Disseminate along with state policy and resource documents relevant to collaboration.
Local administrators, local Interagency Coordinating Councils (ICCs), and other local collaborative teams	Use the manual as a guide for facilitating the development of local collaborative teams. Use the manual as a guide for sustaining or rejuvenating existing local collaborative teams as they address new challenges. Disseminate the manual to all team members to facilitate the building of leadership capacity and team ownership. Disseminate the manual to all team members and ask them to share it with their respective agencies as a resource for both collaborative and other related agency activities.

Overview of CPP Project and Local CPP Teams

The purpose of the Collaborative Planning Project (CPP) for Comprehensive Early Childhood Systems was to facilitate the establishment of local collaborative teams to work on one or more mutually agreed-to challenges associated with putting in place a long-term vision. This vision was locally determined but had to relate in some form to inclusive, quality, comprehensive early care and education services to young children birth through five (or up to age eight) and their families. A CPP facilitator was assigned to work with each team for approximately six sessions, after which each team became self-sustaining—having organized as a team, accomplished at least one concrete task, and created a plan for further collaborations.

Local CPP teams were selected to be representative of urban, rural, and suburban communities. Each team was instructed to include a representative(s) of:

- A school district early childhood/early childhood special education program;
- An Early Intervention program;
- An Early Head Start and/or Head Start program;
- Child care programs;
- Families; and
- Others at the discretion of the community team, depending on the nature of the issues the team intended to address.

The project selected two types of teams for project participation. One set of teams was located all in one state: Rhode Island (RI). The four RI teams were all linked to a statewide early childhood collaboration initiative. That is, an RI state-level interagency task force was in place that had previously negotiated a state interagency agreement among early intervention, education, and Head Start. The task force had also developed a comprehensive interagency TA guide. They had in place an annual statewide training event focusing on early childhood collaboration that was used to showcase CPP and other collaborative teams and to facilitate networking among local communities. The task force

assisted in selecting the following RI CPP teams. CPP Facilitator Peggy Hayden worked with these teams:

Central Falls, RI, CPP Team
Community Description: Inner city/urban
Time frame of project participation:
September 1999–November 2000
Focus during project participation:
Developing strategies to ensure that (1) all agency staff and families have equal access to a common set of information on community resources related to children and their families and (2) families have access to this information either via a key community agency (i.e., the agency with which they are already involved) or via a call to a resource and referral line.

Cranston, RI, CPP Team
Community Description: Suburban community
Also known as a "ring" community because it forms part of the suburban ring around Providence.
Time frame of project participation:
February–November 2000
Focus during project participation:
To (1) establish a "Cranston Cabinet" of key agency decision-makers and (2) develop a universal release of information form.

South Kingstown, RI, CPP Team
Community Description: Suburban
Time frame of project participation:
January–November 2000
Focus during project participation:
To (1) develop mechanisms to assist families and professionals in accessing community services, (2) blend resources to expand early childhood care and education service options for young children and their families, and (3) coordinate and expand parenting programs.

Westerly, RI, CPP Team
Community Description: Suburban/rural
Time frame of project participation:
September 1999–November 2000
Focus during project participation:
To (1) strengthen linkages with physicians to facilitate early identification and referral of children with special needs, and (2) provide training and other supports to increase the awareness of families regarding typical and

atypical development, including how they can support their child's development and access services in the community.

The second set of four teams operated independently in that they were not formally linked to a statewide initiative. However, state agencies helped with team selection. In some instances, state staff also supported local efforts, e.g., attending key meetings or providing policy clarification, training, TA, and/or other resources. CPP Facilitator Linda Frederick worked with these teams.

Crowley, LA, Acadia Parish CPP Team

Community Description: Rural
Time frame of project participation:
1999–2000 school year
Focus during project participation:
To develop a networking system and increase public awareness of all available services for children birth through kindergarten.

Denver, CO, CPP Team

Community Description: Urban
Time frame of project participation:
1998–2000
Focus during project participation:
Issues pertaining to infants and toddlers with special needs and their families under Part C of the Individuals with Disabilities Education Act (IDEA) with particular emphasis on identification and eligibility, service coordination, Individual Family Service Plans (IFSPs), and transition.

Las Vegas, NV, Greater Metropolitan Clark County CPP Team

Community Description: Urban
Time frame of project participation:
August 1999–May 2000
Focus during project participation:
Goals and objectives for service delivery, transition, training, and public awareness issues. The first priority was raising public awareness of community resources for young children and their families.

Longmont, CO, St. Vrain Early Childhood Council CPP Team

Community Description: Suburban/rural
Time frame of project participation:
2000–2001 school year
Focus during project participation:
A collaborative system to ensure (1) the availability and accessibility for early identification of children with special needs or who are at risk for future developmental concerns and (2) family supports.

The teams accomplished much during the five to six sessions that the CPP facilitator was present. Particularly noteworthy is follow-up impact evaluation that reveals that all but two of the eight teams have continued to collaborate on their own in some form for more than a year, sustaining earlier accomplishments and expanding their collaboration in keeping with the visions they initially established when they were formed as a CPP team.

Chapter IX provides detailed profiles on each team, including updates on their status as of Winter 2001–2002 and copies of some of the team products. The accomplishments and overall sustainability of CPP teams are noteworthy. This is attributable to the dedication of team members. It is also the result of an effective model for developing collaborative plans and partnerships to promote systems change related to comprehensive, quality, and inclusive early care and education services for young children and their families.

CPP Model

Legal requirements and research on effective practice underscore the need for and the benefit of services that are comprehensive, high quality, and inclusive to young children with and without special needs (Smith & Rapport, 1999a, 1999b; Smith & Rose, 1993). Unfortunately, our current service delivery system for young children is highly fragmented and duplicates services available through schools, early intervention agencies, Head Start, child care, health and social services, etc. Despite this service array, many young children needing early childhood services go unserved because the demand for services exceeds service capacity. Many children and their families are also underserved, receiving some services from one agency but needing additional services outside of that particular agency's scope. They must either remain underserved or negotiate a maze of service agencies with varied eligibility and service requirements.

Variations may exist in service quality across agencies. Some services may not operate at a level recognized as meeting state or national standards of quality. Even when they do, services operated by varied agencies may have different philosophies and approaches to intervention or instruction (i.e., curricula). This impedes service continuity as children and families transition from one agency to another, thereby making it more difficult for children to achieve the goals established for them by their families and recognized standards for learner outcomes established for children of school age.

Inclusive services are another challenge. Many agencies' services for young children are limited in scope to those funded by single or limited funding streams. They may provide only a narrow range of services or serve only a narrow range of children. For example, many school districts provide special education and related services only to preschool children with disabilities and do not operate programs for preschool children without disabilities. This poses a challenge to districts in providing inclusive services and meeting the legal mandate for preschool special education in the least restrictive environment where children with and without disabilities are educated together to the maximum extent appropriate. Agencies providing early intervention services to infants and toddlers with disabilities face similar challenges related to the mandate for services in natural environments through functional participation in the family's daily activities, routines, and events in everyday life. In order to provide inclusive services and meet these legal mandates, schools and early intervention agencies find it necessary to collaborate with other agencies where such environments are available.

In *Early childhood inclusion policy and systems: What do we know?*, Smith and Rapport (1999a) suggest that collaborative planning at the community level is an alternative for addressing service fragmentation and issues on service quality and inclusion. They state that collaboration:

> . . . *can bring together Head Start, child care, parents, schools and others as appropriate to build together a vision and system of early childhood services for all children. These collaborative efforts can result in better understanding of the various programs, of the needs of families of young children, and of how to meet the diverse needs of all children in the community. These efforts can result in a better and more efficient use of limited resources by promoting sharing and reallocation of space, funds, transportation, personnel training opportunities, etc. And finally, these efforts can result in communication and respect across programs and between programs and families. (p. 13)*

Collaborative approaches to systems change are also supported by *DEC Recommended Practices in Early Intervention/Early Childhood Special Education* in the chapter on Policies, Procedures, and Systems Change (Sandall, McLean, & Smith, 2000). As provided in this chapter, practices should address the following issues:

- Families and professionals shaping policy at the federal, state, and local levels.

- Public policies promoting the use of recommended practices.

- Program policies and administration promoting family participation in decision-making.

- Program policies and administration promoting the use of recommended practices.

- Program policies and administration promoting interagency and interdisciplinary collaboration.

- Program policies, administration, and leadership promoting program evaluation and systems change efforts. (pp. 70–74)

An effective model is needed to help change the early childhood service delivery system from one of fragmented services with a single agency orientation to a system that is comprehensive, quality, and inclusive. However, bringing about such systems change is a challenging task.

Systems change is not an isolated event in which you "change the system" by passing legislation or simply developing policies and procedures. As Fullan (1993) puts it, "You can't mandate what matters" and "the more complex the change, the less you can force it" (p. 22). "Events" such as mandates are important. But, for the desired change to become reality, people must act. Ensuring such actions requires systematically planning, implementing, and evaluating strategies that impact both agencies and individuals who are agency staff and who are the beneficiaries of agency services (Fullan, 1993; Guskey & Huberman, 1995; Senge, 1990). Research (Fullan, 1991; Fullan, 1993; Guskey & Huberman, 1995; Senge, 1990) shows that we must address a variety of system issues such as:

- Having a clear sense of our current context including analysis of those features we would like to change;

- Articulating a "shared vision" that describes what the results of change would look like;

- Providing professional development to ensure that people have the necessary knowledge and skills to enact the change;

- Ensuring adequate fiscal, human, and facility resources;

- Offering change incentives;

- Providing ongoing supports to assist people with change implementation; and

- Monitoring and evaluating the process and impact of change.

Systems change is not accomplished in a "neat," linear, cause-and-effect mode because systems are dynamic and ever evolving (Fullan, 1993; Mintzberg, 1994; Senge, 1990). At the same time systemic changes are being implemented, there must be an effective means of continuous plan review and updates in order to reflect both the learnings from plan implementation and the ever changing context in which the plan is being implemented related to new mandates, staff

turnover, budget cuts, program growth, and so on. In short, planning is not a project "we do" and then "we're done!"

Applying systems change to facilitating comprehensive early childhood systems is complicated, because multiple agencies and consumers make up the system. In reality, it is a system of systems. Promoting change in just one agency can be challenge enough! Change on an interagency basis requires each participating agency to change to some degree both internally and in the way it works with other agencies. To ensure that the change process is meaningful, it must be embedded in and responsive to the needs of participating agencies both individually and collectively.

The Collaborative Planning Project's (CPP) model for planning comprehensive early childhood systems was designed to respond to these various issues. The CPP model (Hayden, Smith, Rapport, & Frederick, 1999) presented in this manual includes the following components:

1. Ensuring leadership commitment, which is described in Chapter III.

2. Establishing a stakeholder team, which is described in Chapters III and IV.

3. Creating a shared vision, which is described in Chapter V.

4. Developing action plans, which is described in Chapter VI.

5. Implementing action plans and allocating resources, which is described in Chapter VII.

6. Evaluating the above components as well as the impact of action plan implementation, which is described in the "Are We There Yet?" section at the end of Chapters III–VII.

7. Providing developmental facilitation, which is described in Chapter II and throughout Chapters III–VII.

The Tour Guide

Facilitator Selection and Role

Initially, an individual should be chosen to serve as team facilitator until the team becomes successfully established. This usually takes several months, i.e., a school year. During this project, CPP staff served as initial facilitators, assisting team members who then assumed the facilitator role when CPP staff left.

The facilitator is "a person who is acceptable to all members of the group," is "substantively neutral," does not have authority over the group, and helps the "group improve the way it identifies and solves problems and makes decisions, in order to increase the group's effectiveness" (Schwarz, 1994, p. 4). It is ideal to have an "outside" facilitator, such as a consultant, technical assistance (TA) staff, or staff from an agency represented on the team but with no vested interest in the team's work. However, a person on the team can serve in this role (e.g., a chair) as long as the team believes this person to be neutral in the way he or she facilitates the team and as long as team facilitation activities are designed so that he or she can step in and out of the facilitator role as needed to also represent his or her constituency. Throughout this manual, the reader will find facilitation tips and activities to support this role.

SOUVENIR

"Starting out with an outside facilitator was helpful, because it helped the team focus on a collective agenda, rather than letting a single agenda dominate."

South Kingstown, RI, CPP Team

As described in the paper *Developmental facilitation: Helping teams promote systems change* (Hayden, Frederick, Smith, & Broudy, 2001a), the term *developmental facilitation* is used to emphasize that facilitation is not a static process. That is, the team experiences various developmental stages (Hayden, Frederick, Smith, & Broudy, 2001a) coinciding with their status in the change process:

1. Team analysis of the current community context;

2. Change initiation when team members lack the confidence, competence, and full commitment needed to institute the change;

3. Growing competence, confidence, and commitment to the change;

4. Full change implementation; and

5. Desired change is now current context

Both the team as a whole and individual members will evolve through these phases of the change process. Facilitator roles and tasks should evolve accordingly as depicted on Figure 1 and described in the remainder of this chapter.

Figure 1
Developmental Facilitation Model
How Facilitators Can Support Teams and Individuals in the Change Process

Change process status	1. Current context	2. Change initiation: Compliance with loss of security and sense of competence	3. Growing competence, confidence, and commitment	4. Full implementation of desired change	5. Desired change achieved—now current context
Team stage and behavior	Forming Reactive	Storming Authoritarian	Norming Social/Casual	Performing Effective teamwork	Transforming Reflecting, refocusing, self-starting
Individual team member impact (C-BAM)	Needs information	Wonders "what's in it for me?"	Implements change mechanically and superficially	Implements change routinely, evaluating outcomes and networking	Seeks ways to improve or replace practice to be even better
Facilitator role	Director Foundation builder	Capacity builder Referee Nominalizer	Task manager Coach Supporter	Delegator Process advisor Cheerleader	Analyst Synthesizer
Facilitator tasks	Create awareness Orient to task Organize	Facilitate sharing of divergent ideas on direction to develop mutual understanding and work toward a shared vision and plan	Support plan implementation Data flow and analysis	Support plan implementation Track outcomes and impact on context Celebrate	Help team reflect on and evaluate strategies used to apply learnings to "new" reality—so future can be built on past successes

(Hayden et al., 2001a, p. 5)

Team Stages and Behavior

Throughout the collaboration process, the facilitator's role is to build the team's capacity. Capacity building includes developing effective interpersonal skills and relationships without which plans and interagency agreements, no matter how well written, can only endure on paper but not in practice (Fisher & Brown, 1988). Particularly for interagency teams, the team may not have worked together in the past or may even have a rocky history. Thus, while all of the members of an interagency team may be high performing individuals, the team itself may not be.

The team will likely go through several stages of team development (Fay & Doyle, 1982):

1. Getting to know each other and their task (forming);

2. Sharing commonalties and differences (storming);

3. Developing common ground and a plan of action (norming);

4. Working together to implement, monitor, and evaluate the plan (performing); and

5. Finally, when the plan is completed, making a decision on whether to continue as a team to address new issues or reconstituting the team as needed (transforming).

It is important to note that these are general stages of evolution. There is no guarantee that a particular team will go through all of these stages in a linear fashion. A variety of variables can cause the team to stall or stop completely in an early stage. Moreover, even teams at a "higher" stage (e.g., norming or performing) can revert to an earlier stage of team development. This may be due to factors such as turnover in team membership (in which they may need to re-form and re-storm in order to re-norm); inadequacy of training, incentives, or resources necessary for making the change work; too many changes being imposed at one time, etc. Finally, there is no set period of time allocated to each of these stages; it varies from team to team. With these caveats, this general framework for team development stages has been found to be helpful in guiding the facilitator's work with the team.

SOUVENIR

"This group performed better with an outside, neutral facilitator. Allegiance and commitment to the group was fragile and needed lots of encouragement. The local stakeholders struggled to develop cohesion and a unique group identity. The team was still learning to be a team, much less trying to facilitate a struggling group."

Greater Metropolitan Clark County Las Vegas, NV, CPP Team

Individual Team Member Impact (C-BAM)

Just as teams go through different stages in dealing with change, so do individuals. According to the Concerns-Based Adoption Model (C-BAM), individuals go through various levels of concerns (motivation), decisions (about what to do), and behaviors (based on their concerns and decisions) in relation to following through on plans and decisions made by the team (Hall, Wallace, & Dossett, 1973). Individuals start by needing information, then wondering "what's in it for me?" If they buy into the changes proposed by the team, they begin implementing those changes mechanically and superficially. As their competence and confidence grows in implementing the change, the new way of doing things becomes routine. New habits replace old habits. As they see that the changes are benefiting them and the people they serve, team members are motivated to continue change implementation, to evaluate the outcomes of their efforts, and to network with others to share ideas. Finally, once the change is fully implemented and is found to be effective, team members will seek ways to improve or replace the new practice to make it even better.

SOUVENIR

"Change takes place one person at a time."

Greater Metropolitan Clark County Las Vegas, NV, CPP Team

Facilitator Role and Tasks

The facilitator supports team members in building their capacity to work together. As the capacity of the team evolves, so does the facilitator's role. The facilitator has a more directive role as the team begins. Over time, the facilitator's role becomes more supportive, letting the team become self-directive so that its long-term success is not dependent on the facilitator.

The facilitator's first role is director and foundation builder. The role then shifts to that of referee and nominalizer to help the team find common ground and make all members feel equal and valued despite their varied roles or job titles (particularly in the early stages). Then, as the team progresses, the role shifts to task management to ensure solidifying the team's plan and initiating its implementation including collecting and analyzing plan implementation data. When the team is able to demonstrate effective teamwork and is fully implementing the plan, the facilitator's role shifts to delegator, process advisor, and cheerleader, helping the team trace outcomes and impact and celebrate its success. Finally, when the team's initial priority(ies) is achieved, the facilitator supports the team's transformation through serving as an analyst and synthesizer to help the team reflect on and evaluate its experiences and determine next steps (Fay & Doyle, 1982; Schwarz, 1994).

SOUVENIR

"The facilitator served as a model for the team, increasing our awareness of the importance of having an agenda, staying focused and on task in meetings, and having minutes to summarize discussion and decisions and to clearly define next steps. We learned a variety of facilitation processes such as visioning; how to assess community strengths, weaknesses, opportunities and threats; how to do action planning as well as how to run meetings in general using processes such as open and round-robin discussion, merging cards on a storyboard flip chart, etc."

Cranston, RI, CPP Team

Throughout the team's evolution, it is critical that the team believes that the planning is focusing on the agenda of the team and not that of the facilitator. Even though the facilitator is in the front of the room, the power is not; the power is *in* the room, within the team members themselves. The facilitator's role is to help the members harness and collectively focus their power.

In doing so, facilitators may feel that they are engaged in a balancing act. Facilitators need to help the team plan comprehensively and strategically to address community needs consistent with a long-term team vision. But, facilitators also need to help team members figure out how they will work together, how each member/agency fits in, and what will be expected of them. Mintzberg (1994) contends that planners (facilitators) tend to be more reflective and patient with the planning process. Facilitators are apt to want to plan more comprehensively and deal with more abstract issues, because that is the "meta-position" from which they view the system. Managers (agency staff and consumers who compose the team) generally view the need for change more narrowly and want to see quick results to address issues with which they deal on a day-to-day basis so that they will feel that their time is being well spent. Successful planning requires both. These needs can be balanced by thinking big and starting small (Fullan, 1993).

If the initial planning process is successful and responsive to immediate needs, team members will see a return on their investment of time and resources. They will be inclined to want to build on that success, tackling additional and more comprehensive issues at a later date. It takes time to build the capacity of teams to work together and to own the planning (Rous, Hemmeter, & Schuster, 1999). But this time investment actually saves time in the long run because it establishes a solid foundation for successful collaboration on plan implementation and it increases the likelihood that team actions will produce meaningful systems change. In short, you must go slow to go fast (Fullan, 1993).

SOUVENIR

"Teams need to be patient at first. In the initial stages, it is very important to learn about each other as agencies, taking time to discuss the services offered by each and the potential opportunities and benefits of collaboration for individual agencies as well as the team/community as a whole. These discussions will assist the team in moving toward a clear understanding of each other and a clear and common goal."

Central Falls, RI, CPP Team

Chapter III

Getting Started

Establishing Shared Leadership Commitment and a Team Structure for Collaboration

The journey toward systems change starts with establishing a shared leadership commitment and a team structure for collaboration. The shared leadership embodies two (2) key elements:

- Agencies represented on the team jointly "own" the team. It is not seen as the team of one agency even though representatives of a single agency may call the first meeting.

- Persons who serve on the team share responsibility for leadership on the team by serving in a variety of roles, e.g., convenor, recorder, timekeeper, persons responsible for various collaborative plan tasks, etc.

Shared leadership is something that will emerge as commitment deepens over time. However, at the outset of the collaboration, some individual or group of persons will need to take a leadership role in initially convening a team of people to address community needs in a collaborative way. In this manual, we will refer to this person(s) as the **convenor**. The convenor will have one or more reasons for forming the team. These may include some external motivation (e.g., a legal mandate, a new grant opportunity, etc.) and/or some internal/community need (e.g., the need to coordinate or expand services or to resolve problems in current collaborative practices).

The convenor can identify this reason for forming a team independently or, preferably, in consultation with other potential team members. Once an initial reason is identified for convening the team, the convenor decides which agencies and/or individuals have an interest in such a collaboration and then proceeds with the tasks outlined in this chapter:

1. Getting shared leadership commitment and recruiting collaborative team participants;

2. Conducting the organizational meeting to get acquainted, assess the current community context, and determine the team's initial focus; and

3. Creating an effective structure for the team's operation including team ground rules.

Chapter IV, a companion to this chapter, will provide more in-depth information about developing meaningful stakeholder relationships and involvement both during the "getting started stage" as well as throughout the journey of collaboration.

Backseat Driving:

Potential Reasons to Convene an Early Childhood Collaborative Team

Start with activities for which agencies need each other. That is, it is difficult or impossible to do these activities as a single agency with no collaboration.

- Transition
- Child find/child outreach
- Developing a communitywide service directory
- Communitywide screening
- Public awareness regarding the benefit of early childhood services
- Formation of a local interagency coordinating council

Getting Shared Leadership Commitment and Recruiting Collaborative Team Participants

Which way to go? *Which agencies should be invited to be involved on the collaborative team?*

Directions: Start with a core team of agencies. Involving agencies representative of the early childhood system does not mean having everyone literally "at the table" as regular members of the collaborative team. Rather, it is advisable to start with a core of key stakeholders who are open to collaboration and who have a legitimate, immediate and direct interest in the reason(s) for which the team is being convened. The core team's role is to serve as the steering committee for the planning process. To ensure that the team's size is manageable for the planning task, **keep the number of core team members to between five and nine, no more than twelve if at all possible** (Daniels, 1986). For example, if the initial reason for convening the team is transition, the convenor might start by inviting those agencies immediately involved in transition, e.g., early intervention, public schools, Head Start, and child care programs.

Then, as the core team discusses issues over time relevant to agencies with a more secondary interest in transition (e.g., health or social services), these agencies can be invited to work with the team on an ad hoc basis when issues of interest to them are on the agenda.

SOUVENIR

"Core team member selection requires consideration of more than team member knowledge and authority related to the agency or interest that they represent. Core team attitudes are also very important. Participants need to be 'ready' both individually and collectively to work together. If they have a negative attitude toward change and toward each other, they are not ready to start the planning process. Instead, it is preferable to find a focus around which a team can be organized with willing and able members, even if that focus is initially limited."

Denver, CO, CPP Team

Backseat Driving:

Typical Core Team Memberships

- School district early childhood/early childhood special education program;
- Early Intervention;
- Early Head Start and/or Head Start;
- Child care programs;
- Families; and
- Others at the discretion of the community team, depending on the nature of the issues the team intends to address.

Which way to go? *How can shared leadership commitment from these agencies be ensured?*

Directions: Seek out commitment from the heads of agencies. In some instances, an agency head will be a regular core team member, e.g., the child care program director, the director of a private non-profit, etc. In many instances, the agency head will appoint a designee whose job is most immediately relevant to the team's focus. For example, the school superintendent will designate the special education or preschool director. At a minimum, the convenor should ensure that the head of each agency represented on the team is (1) aware of the team and its reason for forming and (2) supportive of representatives from his/her agency participating in regular meetings (e.g., monthly). Securing this commitment can be done through the convenor's contact with the agency head or working through the designee.

SOUVENIR

As was typical for CPP teams, the Cranston, RI, CPP Team was composed mostly of middle managers. They wanted an ongoing mechanism to ensure that collaboration would have support "from the top" of their respective agencies. They recommended establishment of the Cranston Cabinet, a group of agency heads and "final" decision-makers: public school superintendent, Comprehensive Community Action Director, mayor, YMCA director, and other key agencies and officials either on a regular or ad hoc basis, e.g., Central Region Early Intervention, police department, library, mental health services, etc. The Cabinet meets 2–4 times a year to:

- Establish interagency teams/committees of middle management and line staff, families, and others, as appropriate, to pursue particular community needs and/or respond to various initiatives that come down from state or federal levels (such as the CPP team);

- Provide input to these teams to help them set direction; and

- Serve as a source of final interagency decisions and commitment to support implementation of these decisions within their respective agencies.

Which way to go? *Which staff from these agencies need to be involved on the team?*

Directions: Core team members should include agency representatives who have decision-making authority or who have ready access to decision-makers. For those team members who are not decision-makers, they should establish protocol with the decision-maker they represent for keeping that decision-maker informed of the team's work and for seeking input and decisions from him or her.

SOUVENIR

A Central Falls, RI, CPP Team commented that "it is critical to get key people involved and committed from the start . . . It's often too difficult to involve direct caregivers, because they are too busy and it's too hard to find substitutes for their daily work. It is better to involve administrators or families on the core team." The majority of the CPP teams included staff that were decision-makers and middle managers rather than line staff due to reasons as cited here. However, some teams did include line staff, often doing so very successfully. One team even met in the evenings on occasion to accommodate the schedules of both line staff and families.

Which way to go? *How can the interests of families be effectively represented on the team?*

Directions: Two or more family representatives should be on the core team to represent consumer perspectives. Ideally, such family members represent a group of families rather than only their individual experiences, e.g., Head Start Policy Council, local school PTA/PTO, an advocacy group, or local advisory council.

Which way to go? *What steps need to be taken to invite potential team members to an organizational meeting?*

Directions: Personal contact such as a one-to-one meeting or a phone call to recruit team members increases the likelihood of involvement. The convenor can use these contacts to learn about various issues that are both motivators and causes of concern related to team involvement.

SOUVENIR

"Change takes place one person at a time, and is often based on the relationship between the change agent and the participants. If we were just starting, I would . . . establish relationships with leaders of each agency and develop a base or foundation for future change. I (needed) in-depth knowledge of resources and politics. Leadership/facilitation (requires) intimate knowledge of (local) system issues."

*Greater Metropolitan Clark County
Las Vegas, NV, CPP Team Chair*

Once personal contacts have been made, a follow-up letter should be sent to confirm the organizational meeting. It is helpful to ask each team member to bring information about his or her agency such as a brochure. The follow-up letter can also request completion of an Agency Profile (see Chapter IV) to provide basic agency information.

Sample Letter

Asking Potential Team Members to Attend the Organizational Meeting

TO:

FROM:

DATE:

RE: Organizational Meeting for Community Collaborative Team

I appreciate your interest in forming a community collaborative team and your willingness to attend our organizational meeting. Our purpose will be to look at ways in which we can work together, ways that will benefit children and families, our individual agencies, and our community at large. Our organizational meeting will be:

Date/Time: _____

Location: _____

To help us prepare for this meeting, I am enclosing:

1. An agenda for our meeting;
2. An Agency Profile form. Please complete this and bring ___ copies to share at our meeting. This will help us get acquainted with the services we each provide. Please feel free to bring any brochures or other materials that seem appropriate;
3. A tentative list of collaborative team members;
4. An RSVP regarding your attendance at this meeting; and
5. Directions to the meeting site.

I look forward to seeing you at our meeting. If you have any questions, please call me at _____.

This form may be reproduced without permission.

RSVP Regarding
Attending Collaborative Team Meeting

Please return this RSVP by _____ (date)
and return it to _____.

Confirmation of Participation

Name: _____

Agency/Constituency: _____

Address: _____

_____

Phone: _____ Fax: _____ E-mail: _____

___ Yes, I will be able to attend this meeting.

___ No, I will not be able to attend, but I am interested in being a member of the team
and wish to be invited to the next meeting.

___ No, I am not interested in being a member of the team at this time.

Comments: _____

_____

This form may be reproduced without permission.

Which way to go? *What do you do if one or more of the agencies you think need to be on the team refuses to participate?*

Directions: If one or two agencies choose not to participate on the team, don't let that prevent the team from collaborating. Rather, choose a common issue for collaboration that is relevant to those interested in collaboration. Then, as the team progresses, keep the uninvolved agencies informed via copies of minutes or related team

SOUVENIR

"If someone wasn't on board, then we didn't stop but proceeded anyway. We made sure that everyone on the team was enthusiastic."

Westerly, RI, CPP Team

products, periodic phone calls, or personal contacts. Such information may ultimately persuade them to become part of the collaboration.

Conducting the Organizational Meeting to Get Acquainted, Assess the Current Community Context, and Determine the Team's Initial Focus

Which way to go? *Who will facilitate and take minutes at the first meeting?*

Directions: The convenor should make arrangements in advance for someone to facilitate and record/take minutes at the initial meeting. Facilitator and recorder roles can be assumed by the convenor and other team members. The convenor can also make arrangements to have a neutral person (nonteam member) serve as facilitator (see Chapter II). At the organizational meeting, the team will make decisions about who will serve in these roles on an ongoing basis.

Which way to go? *Where will the meeting be held?*

Directions: Any meeting of the team should be held in a pleasant meeting space that accommodates working around a table or tables arranged in a square or "U." Team members need to easily see and converse with each other. The room should be reasonably private (i.e., with no interruptions and few people coming in and out). There needs to be enough wall space for posting flip charts on the wall. Arrange for a flip chart on a stand for recording. Ask a team member to bring light refreshments. (The more people have a role to play in the meeting, the more they will feel truly involved.) Make sure everyone knows directions to the meeting site.

Which way to go? *What are key issues that need to be addressed at the organizational meeting? How much time should be allocated?*

Directions: The purposes of the initial meeting are to help the team:

1. Become acquainted with each other (sharing of agency information);

2. Assess where they are now (current community context);

3. Decide where they would like to go as a team (initial team focus); and

4. Establish how they will work together (ground rules).

A sample Collaborative Team Organizational Meeting Agenda is provided here and is followed by complete explanations of the activities listed on this agenda. The agenda has been developed with a four-hour time frame in mind. This time frame is approximate. The actual time needed to carry out agenda activities will be affected by the number of people attending, how well they know each other, and the degree of consensus about community needs. Depending on team member availability to meet, it may be necessary to cover the activities in this agenda over two meetings.

Collaborative Team
Organizational Meeting Agenda

Date/Time: _____

Location: _____

What to Bring

1. This agenda
2. A completed agency profile, brochures, and other related information (enough to share)

Meeting Purposes: The team will have:

1. A common understanding of the agencies represented at this meeting
2. An identification of the community's strengths, weaknesses, opportunities, and threats
3. Confirmation of the team's focus
4. Confirmation of team ground rules, including meeting schedule and membership
5. A plan for next steps

Agenda

8:30   Welcome, introductions, and agenda review—Team Convenor(s)

8:45   Learning about each other: Reviewing agency profiles with Q & A

10:00   Break

10:15   Assessing community strengths, weaknesses, opportunities, and threats (SWOTS)

10:45   Confirming the team's focus based on agency profiles and our SWOTS
Based on what we have just discussed, what particular topic(s) or focus should this team pursue that would benefit children and families, the agencies represented here, and the community at large.

11:15   Establishing our ground rules: Reviewing and editing the sample, and confirming our team mailing list

Noon   Next Steps: Follow-up after this meeting and plans for next meeting

12:15   Evaluating our time together: Team discussion about what made the meeting effective and things we could do to improve it

12:30   Adjourn

This form may be reproduced without permission.

Which way to go? *What are strategies for helping team members develop a common understanding of the services provided by the agencies represented on the team?*

Directions: At the organizational meeting, review the agency profiles, brochures, and related information that members have brought to share to help them get acquainted with each other. Even though agencies may have worked together in various ways in the past, they benefit from sharing information about each other.

Backseat Driving:

Tips on Helping Team Members Get Acquainted With Each Other

- Start the meeting with agency information sharing. This allows all members to participate and feel involved from the very beginning of the meeting, promoting a sense of "our" meeting rather than "the convenor's" meeting.

- Reviewing agency information helps the team establish a common knowledge base of early childhood community resources.

- Have the team recorder keep a file of team profiles to share with new members as they are added to the team and to have available as a resource to the team (e.g., for brochure or service directory development).

- For tips on helping team members get acquainted as individuals, see Chapter IV.

SOUVENIR

The St. Vrain Early Childhood CPP Team, Longmont, CO, organized agency information into a resource matrix for the team to use in analyzing gaps in resources and identifying community needs. This led to this observation by one team member, "The community of early childhood systems in St. Vrain is like an old house that has been remodeled and revamped continuously over the years until it has too many rooms. It's hard for a family to find their way from one room to another. We need to take out some of the walls and open it up and make it easy to negotiate. We need to focus on quality as well as practicality as we remodel once again."

Which way to go? *What are strategies for helping team members evaluate current early childhood services in the community as a prelimi-*

nary step to deciding the focus that the team wants to take?

Directions: Agency information sharing sets the scene for the next activity on the organizational meeting agenda—an assessment of the community's current context related to early childhood services. A helpful process for assessing the community's early childhood service system is through an analysis of community strengths, weaknesses, opportunities, and threats—SWOTs (Mintzberg, 1994; Pfeiffer, Goodstein, & Nolan, 1989; Bryson, 1988). The team examines:

- Both strengths and weaknesses—Current issues reflecting perspectives of staff and consumers; existing mandates, policies, and procedures; demographic information; recent successes and challenges; data on services; staffing patterns; and

- Both opportunities and threats—Issues "on the horizon" such as potential funding sources, new mandates, competition, and increased demand for services/waiting lists.

This assessment helps team members see where they have common strengths and needs and how collaboration might be useful to them individually and collectively. If the team's initial focus/topic of collaboration has not been determined in advance of the organizational meeting, this assessment can help lead the team to making this decision. If the focus has already been determined, the SWOT activity can help to further define that focus. Ultimately, the assessment of the community's current context will serve as the foundation for articulating the team's vision as described in Chapter V. (NOTE: Some teams enjoy becoming SWOT teams to "attack" community issues. Other teams prefer replacing the word *weaknesses* with *concerns*, making community assessment a SCOT process.)

SOUVENIR

Assessing community needs resulted in one Denver, CO, CPP Team member concluding that "the system which was intended to be a 'funnel' for service access has evolved into a 'colander'!" Insights such as these helped the team plan strategies to take them toward their focus and vision for service coordination.

Backseat Driving:

Tips for Using a Storyboard

Many activities in this manual call for the use of a **storyboard**. This is created using flip chart paper taped on the wall, usually two (2) or more overlapping pages to make a large working surface. Team members record ideas on note cards or sticky notes and post these ideas on the storyboard for team review and "moving around" on the storyboard to merge/group common ideas or organize ideas under various headings. Team members should use markers for recording ideas so that ideas can be seen on the storyboard from a distance. Using a storyboard generates a lot of ideas in a short amount of time. It facilitates team building, because team members generate many of the same ideas. Redundancy is good, because it reflects consensus and members can readily see this "common ground" on the storyboard.

Using the Storyboard With Temporary Adhesive and Note Cards: Spray posted chart pages with a temporary spray adhesive (e.g., 3M™ Spray Mount™ Artist's Adhesive). The spray makes the paper feel like the sticky part of a sticky note. Items posted will not stick permanently. One can post note cards or similar materials and then move them around on the storyboard. 5" x 8" note cards are preferred, because they are easier to see from a distance.

Using the Storyboard With Sticky Notes: Leave the chart pages unsprayed. Place 4" x 6" sticky notes on the storyboard and then move these around as needed for the activity.

Using Headings for Merging Ideas:

- Some activities in this manual start with headings posted on the storyboard. Examples are the SWOT activity with headings for Strengths, Weaknesses, Opportunities, and Threats, and later in this manual, Action Planning with headings for strategies/action steps, resources, people, timeline, and outcomes. The facilitator asks team members to post ideas under the appropriate heading. The facilitator then leads the team in merging common ideas in columns under each heading by either grouping or eliminating redundant ideas.

- Some activities start with no preset headings, e.g., the "Activity to Determine a Team's Initial Focus" (which appears later in this chapter) and the "Visioning Activity" (which appears in Chapter IV). Team members post ideas on a blank storyboard. Then, common ideas are merged into vertical columns. A blank card or sticky note on which a heading will be written is placed at the top of each column. Once all columns are set, the facilitator leads the team in deciding the primary theme or concept to serve as the heading for each column. Headings then become key elements of the team's initial focus or the team's vision. If desired, ideas under each heading can be used as is or edited as explanation for each key element/heading.

Merging/Grouping Common Ideas (Note Cards or Sticky Notes) Into Columns: It is preferable to merge or group common ideas into vertical columns so that the cards or notes touch but do not overlap. Upon completion of the activity, the recorder runs a piece of scotch tape from the top to the bottom of the column of cards or sticky notes. This allows the whole column to be removed for easy transport and use by the person transcribing the minutes or for bringing the column back to a future meeting.

Activity

Assessing Your Community's Strengths, Weaknesses, Opportunities, and Threats

"Making You a SWOT Team to Attack Community Issues"

1. Appoint a facilitator, recorder, and timekeeper.

2. The **recorder** sets up a storyboard with the following four columns:

   <u>S</u>trengths <u>W</u>eaknesses <u>O</u>pportunities <u>T</u>hreats

3. Ask **each team member** to identify what he or she sees as their community's major strengths, weaknesses, opportunities, and threats. He or she should write these on 5" x 8" note cards* with a marker—one idea per card. When through, he or she should post cards under the appropriate columns on the storyboard.

4. Starting with Strengths, the **facilitator** leads the team in "merging" common ideas under this column on the storyboard. As groupings are developed, a name or title for each grouping is identified that summarizes the grouping. For example, there may be multiple groupings of strengths, each with its own name or title.

5. The **facilitator** continues to help the team with the merging activity until all columns are completed.

6. This activity should take approximately 30–45 minutes. The **timekeeper** helps the team track its time, reminding them periodically of how much time is left.

* This activity calls for note cards. It can also be done using a storyboard with sticky notes as described in the "Backseat Driving: Tips for Using a Storyboard" section previously in this chapter.

This activity may be reproduced without permission.

Which way to go? *How does the team decide on a focus or basic direction to which all members are willing to commit and devote time and effort?*

Directions: The team should confirm the initial focus or team direction as soon as possible. Deciding on this initial focus is key. It helps make collaboration more concrete, making it possible for people to name the reason they are collaborating. This will increase the likelihood that attending team meetings will be meaningful to members.

> **"We focused on problems that kept bothering us . . . year after year—cyclical situations that needed to end."**
>
> *Westerly, RI, CPP Team*

As discussed earlier in this chapter, this focus may be narrow (transition or child find) or broad (establishing a comprehensive early childhood system). The focus will sometimes be determined prior to the organizational meeting as an outgrowth of the convenor's personal contacts. In other instances, the team focus may emerge from the team's assessment of the current context at the organizational meeting. Sometimes, the focus will not become clear until after visioning has taken place and the focus emerges as one or more priority challenges to be addressed via action planning.

If the team's initial focus is not named prior to the organizational meeting or if it does not become fairly self-evident to team members as a result of the community context assessment, the team may find it helpful to use the following activity for this purpose.

Activity

Activity to Determine a Team's Initial Focus

Focus Question: Based on what we have learned through our discussion of our agency profiles and our SWOTS, what particular topic(s) or focus should this team pursue as its initial focus to benefit children and families, the agencies represented here, and the community at large?

1. Appoint a facilitator, recorder, and timekeeper.

2. The **recorder** sets up a storyboard labeled "Our Team Focus." The focus question is written on flip chart paper and posted beside the storyboard.

3. **Each team member** identifies 1–3 answers to the focus question, recording one answer per sticky note* with a marker.

4. **Each team member** posts all sticky notes on chart.

5. **Facilitator** rereads the focus question to the team and leads them in merging similar ideas into groups, arranging sticky notes in vertical columns with a blank sticky note at the top of each column.

6. The **recorder** notes the primary theme or concept of each column on the blank sticky note at the top of each column. These themes become the elements describing the focus the team wants to take.

7. The **facilitator** leads the team in deciding which of the theme/column(s) to pursue as its initial focus or direction. It is recommended that the team start with one primary focus and make note of the other ideas generated for future reference. Then, when the initial focus is achieved, they can reconsider the other ideas generated, building on the success of initial accomplishments.

8. The **timekeeper** helps the team track time (30 minutes).

This activity calls for sticky notes. It can also be done using a storyboard with note cards as described in the "Backseat Driving: Tips for Using a Storyboard" section previously in this chapter.

This activity may be reproduced without permission.

Creating an Effective Structure for the Team's Operation Including Team Ground Rules

At its first meeting(s), the team should negotiate ground rules to ensure that it has an effective operating structure. These ground rules, in effect, constitute criteria for judging how effectively members work together as a team. It is helpful to provide a sample of basic ground rules that the team can adapt to meet its needs rather than starting from scratch. Ground rules should address the following issues.

Which way to go? *Who will be the core team members? What agencies will be involved on an ad hoc basis?*

Directions: Having a decision on the team's basic focus helps the team decide on team membership, that is, whom they need on a regular and ad hoc basis to address this focus (see Chapter IV for an in-depth discussion of this issue).

> "At the initial meeting, many agencies were represented. After the team narrowed its focus and began its actual work, there was some level of 'fallout' of membership. In retrospect, we realized that this is a natural and evolutionary thing. That is, once the focus is solidified, initial participants can decide whether or not they are willing or able to remain involved. This results in a core team of people who are truly committed and who are able to fully participate in team activities. Those individuals for whom the team has only limited relevance can then be involved as 'contributing/ad hoc' members as needed."
>
> *South Kingstown, RI, CPP Team*

Which way to go? *What are key roles on the team that need to be filled to ensure that as many team members as possible are actively involved in the team's operation?*

Directions: Have a leadership structure with clarified roles (e.g., convenor, facilitator, recorder). Team members should all know and be able to carry out their respective roles. Have a schedule for leadership election and rotation. Most teams choose to do this on an annual basis. Select team leaders who are perceived to be fair by all participants, and who will lead the group as a community team and not as a vehicle for promoting his or her own agency agenda. Team leaders and members should have or develop good skills related to facilitating meetings, problem solving, conflict resolution, etc.

SOUVENIR

"It is also important to have shared responsibility for key team tasks, including convening and facilitating the sessions, taking and disseminating minutes as well as carrying out the team's action plan."

Cranston, RI, CPP Team

Which way to go? *What is an effective and easy-to-use format for meeting minutes? What are recommended timelines and distribution strategies for minutes?*

Directions: Use minutes to document meetings. These are the team's record for immediate and future reference. They help promote a common understanding of what took place both for those in attendance and those absent. Minutes should not be a verbatim transcript. Rather, minutes should identify:

- Those in attendance;
- Why the meeting was held;
- A summary of key discussions and decisions;
- Specific next steps for follow-through by team members; and
- Plans for the next meeting (see the following Collaborative Planning Team Minutes Shell).

Although plans for the next meeting are made at the end of the meeting, it is helpful to identify these plans on the first page of the minutes. Doing so will immediately focus team member attention on when and where they need to be for the next meeting, thereby eliminating the need for a cover memo for the minutes or a notice of the next meeting. Minutes should be circulated promptly, within one to two weeks after the meeting, so that team members have "next steps" reminders and absent members can have quick feedback on meeting outcomes. Minutes can be circulated in hard copy or via e-mail.

Collaborative Planning Team Minutes Shell

Date: _____

In attendance: _____

Next Meeting Plans: _____

Date and Time: _____

Location: _____

Purposes: _____

Issue I   Summary of discussion and decisions on the topic of _____

Issue II   Summary of discussion and decisions on the topic of _____

Issue III   Summary of discussion and decisions on the topic of _____
(Add other issues headings if more are needed depending on the meeting agenda.)

Issue IV   Plan for next steps including communicating, as needed, with other stakeholders including people within the agencies represented on the team.

This form may be reproduced without permission.

Which way to go? *What authority does the team have? Can the team make decisions independent of the agencies represented on the team? What will be done if the team cannot agree?*

Directions: Clarify the team's authority and collaborative decision-making process. The team needs to decide on the degree to which it has authority to make decisions. Depending on the nature of the team this may include having:

- Agency representatives authorized to participate in and make decisions affecting their agencies (that is, the team is free to decide);

OR

- A collaborative decision-making process responsive to the decision-making processes of member agencies' chains of command as well as to collaborative needs (that is, team members must get the approval of their respective "bosses" prior to the team making a final decision);

OR

• Some combination thereof. There may be some topics on which the team will have the authority to decide and others that will require the approval of member agencies' chains of command. See also the Chapter IV section, "Fully Engaging a Variety of Stakeholders."

Which way to go? *When and where will team meetings regularly take place? What are guidelines for effective meeting operation?*

Directions: Establish a regular meeting date, time, and location. Monthly meetings of approximately 2–3 hours are recommended. Members may find it more convenient to consistently meet at one location. On the other hand, rotating the meeting location promotes cross-program visitation and team ownership of the agency hosting the team. It helps people to both plan ahead and to remember meeting dates if the time and date are consistent (e.g., third Tuesday, second Wednesday, etc.).

Pay attention to basic standards for effective meetings. Each meeting should have a clear and purposeful agenda with mutually agreed to outcomes clarifying what the team wants to know, have, or be able to do by the time the meeting is over. At the end of each meeting, outcomes should be established for the next meeting so that people have direction about what will happen next and can identify interim steps that will need to be taken to prepare. The meeting should adhere to meeting starting and ending times, adjusting agenda time as needed but making every effort to conclude discussion of each agenda item within the time set.

Backseat Driving:

Tips for Using a Parking Lot to Keep Teams on Task

A major role of the facilitator is to help the team stay on task in order to achieve the outcomes established for the meeting. However, discussion may sometimes sidetrack the team from the purpose of this particular meeting.

• As part of ground rules negotiation, acknowledge that sidetracking will inevitably occur.

• Establish a "Parking Lot" to temporarily "park" ideas that may interfere with being able to get to the destination for the day (meeting outcomes). A Parking Lot is a flip chart on which to record off-track ideas.

• Rather than labeling this as "bad behavior," explain that people are creative thinkers and "off-track" ideas are frequently the result of linking one idea to a new idea. This will help prevent people from feeling punished when their ideas are put in the Parking Lot.

• When the team begins to get off-track, ask if this is something that should be placed in the Parking Lot. If they agree, record it there. If they disagree, set a time limit for discussing the issue, noting that the team may need to adjust its agenda to accommodate this "new" discussion. Agenda adjustment may necessitate not getting to everything on the original agenda.

• At the end of the meeting, review the Parking Lot. If appropriate, schedule the issue(s) noted there as an agenda item for an upcoming meeting. In most instances, items in the Parking Lot will be viewed as creative thinking that can remain in "Long Term Parking."

• A Parking Lot is a very helpful meeting management tool. It also results in building team member capacity to monitor their own behavior and to stay focused. In time, team members will put their own ideas in the Parking Lot when they realize that they are getting off-track.

Which way to go? *What will the team do about absentees?*

Directions: Decide what to do if people miss meetings. Is the absent member responsible for catching up? Will each member have a "buddy" with whom to check? Should they check with the convenor? Will decisions and discussions from a previous meeting be rehashed with absent members?

All members should advise the convenor if they are going to miss a meeting. If a member misses more than two consecutive meetings, don't just "wonder where they are." Inaction may lead to negative consequences such as that agency being unrepresented on the team or erosion of team morale due to people not attending. Instead, take action. Have a team member contact the absent person to inquire about his or her ability to participate on the team. Is the absence a logistics issue (e.g., meeting time or location), a temporary circumstance, or has that individual's situation changed to the extent that they are no longer able to be a regular core team member? Does that person no longer see the team as relevant? What might be done to make the team more relevant? Is a lack of relevance true for that individual alone or for his or her agency as a whole? Is there someone else in that agency that might be better able to attend? If this situation is only temporary, brainstorm strategies with that absent team member for keeping that agency in the loop as an interim measure.

Which way to go? *How will the team handle interpersonal dynamics in meetings? What supports will be in place for building positive team relationships?*

Directions: Decide how to handle interpersonal dynamics in meetings. Provide opportunities for participants to get to know each other as individuals. Building people-to-people relationships has a major positive impact on collaborative relationships and should be built into team activities, e.g., coffee prior to meeting, lunching together before or after a meeting, joint projects, etc. An in-depth discussion of these issues appears in Chapter IV, "Developing Strong Teams Built on Effective People-to-People Relationships."

SOUVENIR

"Ground rules made the meetings a 'safe' place where we could openly discuss difficult issues."

Denver, CO, CPP Team

Which way to go? *How will the team members communicate with others in their respective agencies, including their respective agency chains of command, line staff, and families? What strategies will be used to ensure ongoing information exchange both to share information and to solicit input from a variety of stakeholders? How will the team communicate with other key agencies/stakeholders in the community that are not represented on the team?*

Directions: Discuss the involvement of key stakeholders and respective agency chains of command, line staff, and families. Develop strategies to ensure ongoing information exchange both to share information and to solicit input from a variety of stakeholders. Decide how the team will communicate with other key agencies/stakeholders in the community that are not represented on the team. An in-depth discussion of these issues appears in Chapter IV, "Fully Engaging a Variety of Stakeholders."

Which way to go? *How will the team orient new team members so that they feel welcomed on the team and can be effective contributors?*

Directions: Develop strategies to involve new members so that they feel welcomed on the team and can be effective contributors. These might include having an orientation session for new members, assigning a mentor or buddy to support the new member during initial team participation, and providing a notebook or folder of team products and artifacts such as minutes, membership lists, ground rules, etc.

Sample Ground Rules for the Team to Adapt as Appropriate

Team Name: _____

Team Membership and Roles

1. **Agencies Representative/Individual Participant**—Participates fully. Communicates with the constituencies he/she represents. To keep the team manageable, the number of participants should be five to nine (12 at the most).

   Agency _____ *Who* _____

   Agency _____ *Who* _____

   Agency _____ *Who* _____

   Agency _____ *Who* _____

   Agency _____ *Who* _____

2. **Convenor**—Handles meeting logistics and serves as primary contact for the team. This role may be shared. *Who:* _____

3. **Facilitator**—Leads team meetings in a way that is perceived to be fair, helping the team stay focused and supporting relationship-building needed for effective work. This role may be shared. It may also be the same person as the convenor. Or the convenor and facilitator may be viewed as co-chairs. *Who:*_____

4. **Recorder**—Takes minutes and disseminates to team. If needed, helps facilitator during meeting by recording on flip charts, etc. Maintains team's "master" file or notebook. *Who:* _____

5. **Timekeeper**—Keeps track of time allotments on the agenda and reminds team of the time remaining for each agenda item so that the team can complete items in a timely manner OR adjust agenda as needed. *Who:* _____

6. **Other Community Members**—Not necessarily on team as regular members but involved on an "ad hoc/as needed basis" via survey, interviews, special projects, etc. to accomplish particular tasks.

   *Agency:*_____ *Who:* _____

   Agency _____ *Who* _____

This form may be reproduced without permission.

Sample Ground Rules for the Team to Adapt as Appropriate (continued)

Decision-Making Process

1. We will use consensus. *Consensus* as used here means modified consensus, adhering to the test of "can we live with the proposed idea and publicly support it?" If not, what needs to be changed so that we can?

2. If we cannot achieve consensus on an item, we will (choose one or more):

   ____ Not include it in our plan. "When in doubt, leave it out."

   ____ Take a vote (by member or by agency?).

   ____ Refer this to the respective agency heads of the agencies we represent for decisions, providing for them the various perspectives on this team

   ____ Other (specify):

3. Other rules at the team's discretion:

Meeting Minutes

1. Minutes will be circulated promptly, within one to two weeks after the meeting so that team members have "next steps" reminders and absent members can have quick feedback on meeting outcomes.

2. Minutes will be circulated (check one) ____ in hard copy or ____ via email.

3. Other rules at the team's discretion:

Meeting Logistics

1. Start and end on time.

2. Stay outcome focused using a Parking Lot flip chart on which to record/"park" good ideas not directly related to stated meeting outcomes, i.e., ideas that might get us off task.

3. Meeting Logistics
   - Regular meeting dates and times:
   - Meeting location(s):

4. Maximize our time together and between meetings.

5. Other rules at the team's discretion:

This form may be reproduced without permission.

**Sample Ground Rules for the Team
to Adapt as Appropriate (continued)**

Attendance

1. Attend team meetings regularly.
2. Contact another member for follow-up if a meeting is missed.
3. Other rules at the team's discretion:

Interactions

1. Be realistic; respect others' right to say no.
2. Share ideas and air time. All ideas have value—even ones with which we disagree.
3. Honor confidentiality. What you say here, stays here.
4. Other rules at the team's discretion:

Communicating With Others in Our Agency and Community

1. Communicate with respective agency decision-makers regarding team recommendations:

   _____

2. Communicate with agency decision-makers to ensure they are "in the loop," and supportive/not blocking: _____

3. Communicate with line staff for input as we develop, implement, and evaluate our efforts to make sure that any procedures or activities affecting them will be relevant:

   _____

4. Communicate with families for input as we develop, implement, and evaluate our efforts to make sure that any procedures or activities affecting them will be relevant:

   _____

5. Communicate with others in the community with an indirect interest in our efforts:

   _____

Orientation of New Members

1. Identify a team member to orient each new member and to be that person's "buddy" during the first year on the team.
2. Provide a notebook or file of team orientation materials.
3. Other rules at the team's discretion:

This form may be reproduced without permission.

SOUVENIR

Crowley, LA, Acadia Parish CPP Team Ground Rules (edited slightly for inclusion in this manual)

Team Purpose: *To develop shared vision and plan for comprehensive early childhood systems in Acadia Parish, birth through kindergarten.*

Members: Child Search staff, Even Start staff, Head Start staff, Migrant Program staff, parents, public school staff, school board member, Title I staff.

Roles: The convenor will convene meetings and ask for assistance as needed. CPP staff will facilitate four meetings and provide technical assistance for one year. She will serve as the initial recorder with this role then being assumed by a team member.

Meeting Logistics: The team will meet the first Thursday of each month from 8:30–11:30, rotating meeting sites among agencies.

Decisions: Will be made by consensus.

Communication With Key Stakeholders: Results of this team will be reported to the Louisiana Department of Education as well as being cited as part of the national CPP project. Individual team members will promote task force efforts throughout the community and connect with related efforts like IACADIA, Acadia Resource Network, School Aged Child Care Initiative, and other civic organizations.

Attendance: All participants are asked to make a personal commitment to this effort. Anyone missing a meeting will be contacted and updated by a fellow team member.

Are We There Yet?

Advice on helping teams evaluate their progress and evolve to the next stage.

In establishing the team structure, it is beneficial to end each meeting by having the team reflect on and evaluate the session. Frequently, this ends up being an evaluation of the facilitator. Instead, the facilitator should help the team learn to evaluate itself related to how it is working together and what it is accomplishing. This will help the team develop ownership of the team and how well it operates. It will also cultivate the team's attention to the need for effective meetings and emphasize that they all play key roles in operating as an effective team.

- Team meeting evaluation can be done in writing or as a conversation. Even if done in writing, it is recommended that this individual written reflection be followed by a team dialogue to promote shared understanding of how the team is operating and the generation of team ideas to resolve any operational problems. Methods for doing so include:

  - Reviewing the degree to which the team is adhering to its ground rules;

  - Asking the team to identify pluses and wishes, that is, what contributed to making this a successful meeting (pluses) and what do they wish done differently (wishes for the next meeting); or

  - Have a guided discussion of (1) What did we accomplish today? (2) What helped us? (3) How could our time together have been improved? and (4) What are our reactions to our direction?

SOUVENIR

The St. Vrain Early Childhood Council CPP Team, Longmont, CO, has ended some of its meetings by discussing as a team the following:

I appreciated . . .

I liked . . .

I am concerned about . . .

I wish/hope we . . .

As the team concludes this organizational phase, it should ask itself the following questions related to team organization:

1. Did the team accomplish the outcomes intended at the organizational meeting(s)? Was there good attendance and participation?

2. Do members have a common understanding of the agencies represented on the team?

3. Do members have a common understanding of the current community context related to early childhood services?

4. Does the team have an initial focus that appears to be meaningful to all team members?

5. Are members expressing hope about the potential of this team?

6. Does the team have an effective set of ground rules? Is it starting to operate consistently with these rules?

7. Do members find team meetings to be a good use of their time?

Chapter IV lists questions relevant to team member relationships and buy-in.

Fellow Travelers for the Journey

Developing Meaningful Stakeholder Relationships and Involvement

Chapter III discussed getting started by establishing shared leadership commitment and a team structure for collaboration. These are the "tasks" of organizing an effective collaborative team. This chapter discusses commitment building, group dynamics, and people-to-people relationship issues associated with those who have a stake in what the team does. This manual will refer to these people as **stakeholders**. They include:

- Agency decision-makers who will need to approve and, in some instances, finance their agency's involvement in collaborative plans (depending on the nature of those plans);

- Agency administrative and direct service staff who will ultimately be asked to implement the activities resulting from the collaborative team's planning; and

- Consumers (children and families) who will be impacted by the collaborative plan.

Comprehensive, quality, collaborative, inclusive services are a common goal for people associated with early childhood. However, translating this value into action is often challenging. This is particularly true when stakeholders begin discussing actual commitments of time and resources to collaborative endeavors or changes that individuals or agencies may need to make in order to accomplish collaborative goals.

As a result, cultivating stakeholder commitment is actually a process that most often occurs over time, moving from commitment in theory to commitment in practice. It requires that **team members perceive collaborative activities as meeting one or more of their own needs and, in so doing, broader community goals**. Team members must feel trusted, accepted, and valued as a result of working together. They must also have confidence that this team can tackle challenges and produce positive results, a learning that comes with experience in doing so. Fullan (1993) reinforces the concept that true commitment is not something teams start with but rather is an outcome of people interacting as a team over time, resulting in shared "learning that arises from full engagement in solving problems" together (p. 31).

This chapter addresses the following tasks that teams should undertake in order to develop meaningful stakeholder relationships and involvement:

1. Fostering team member commitment;

2. Fully engaging a variety of stakeholders; and

3. Developing strong teams built on effective people-to-people relationships.

Fostering Team Member Commitment

Which way to go? *Has the team's intention to collaborate come about because of external factors? Have they been told by someone else that they must collaborate (e.g., a state or federal mandate)? Do federal and state legal requirements, grants, or other resources influence collaborative efforts?*

Directions: Sometimes, teams are brought together by some external legal requirement such as the need for an interagency agreement or policy on a particular issue. If this is the case, the facilitator should help the team review the requirement to develop common understanding and identify any commonalties and differences among various agencies related to that requirement. The facilitator should also help the team determine how they can comply with requirements in a way that will be beneficial and relevant to the various team members and their constituencies.

In other cases, teams are brought together because of the availability of funding for some type of project. Sometimes, this process becomes one of identifying how various agencies will support the community agency that will ultimately serve as fiscal agent for the project. That is, although various agencies are involved, the focus is really on one agency. Instead, the team should consider using this as an opportunity for a truly collaborative project by having the facilitator help the team identify common needs across agencies that can be addressed through the grant.

In both of these examples, the critical point is helping the team expand their motivation to be both external (meeting someone else's mandate or needs) and internal (meeting their own needs). Motivation is closely linked to fostering commitment, because people are more likely to commit to things that they perceive meet their own needs.

SOUVENIR

External motivation for CPP teams included the following:

- **The Rhode Island Early Childhood Interagency Task Force recruited four teams using a Request for Proposal process integrating CPP goals with task force goals. The Task Force used their annual statewide meeting to showcase CPP teams and to facilitate networking among CPP and other collaborative teams. State staff presented at the organizational meetings for two of the teams and attended a CPP team meeting with the local board of education in another. State staff and the regional Head Start staff were available for direction on policy clarification and resource location. The South Kingstown, RI, CPP Team reinforced the benefit of being part of a state initiative on collaboration by commenting, "The facilitator helped the team see the bigger picture, sharing information on recommended practice, national trends and models, and what CPP teams in other RI communities were doing. This helped the team learn from others and 'not feel alone' but rather feel empowered as part of a national scene."**

- **State staff in Colorado, Louisiana, and Nevada helped the project select local sites in their states. They attended organizational meetings for most teams and were available in varying degrees for direction on policy clarification and resource location. The Denver, CO, CPP Team noted, "It really helped us to have state and local representatives of each agency together at our first meeting. It gave us 'authority' while input from direct service providers and families gave us 'authenticity.'"**

Which way to go? *Has the intention to collaborate come about because of internal factors based on local community needs? Is this one person/ agency's idea or does there seem to be general agreement on the need to collaborate? What needs do individual team members and their constituencies have for which collaboration is a means to an end rather than an end in itself? Why would people find it beneficial to spend already limited time working together? How can the facilitator help team members move from being mentally tuned into the "radio station" WIIFM (What's In It For Me) into WIIFMC (What's In It For My Community)?*

Directions: No matter whether externally or internally motivated, the facilitator can foster team commitment by helping the team identify common needs on which to base its goals. Activities described in other chapters are tools for doing this: Assessing Your Community's Strengths, Weaknesses, Opportunities, and Threats (in Chapter III); Activity to Determine a Team's Initial Focus (in Chapter III); Visioning Activity (in Chapter V); Activity to Identify Challenges the Team Will Address via Action Planning (in Chapter VI). Using these activities fosters commitment to team plans, because it results in setting team priorities through the input of all individual members. Having all team members as true partners in planning for "new work" or changes that they will ultimately have to make as a result of team plans will result in them being more ready and willing to actually implement these plans. Without this level of commitment based on a sense on perceived benefit, the team's plan will likely be not much more than words on paper.

Backseat Driving:
Tips on Fostering Commitment

- People will initially focus on their own agendas. This is normal; don't condemn them. Rather, seek to find common ground among individual agendas. In so doing, people will buy into collaborative activities that meet one of their own needs as well as a community need. This increases the likelihood that the collaborative team will be relevant to them and worth their time. It helps to foster true commitment.

- Convert "me" mentality to "we" mentality. Typical losers of the "us" and "them" mentalities are the children and families we are all here to serve. Ask team members to evaluate priorities or strategies under consideration by responding to two questions: (1) What's In It For Me—WIIFM? and (2) What's In It For My Community—WIIFMC?

- Give all team members meaningful tasks so that the workload is evenly distributed and so that all members have a reason to be at the meeting. Sometimes these meeting tasks relate to reports, investigations, action plan implementation, resource materials, refreshments, or other "next steps" resulting from previous meetings. Sometimes these are actual team roles as established in the team's ground rules, e.g., facilitator, convenor, recorder, timekeeper, or mentor of a new member.

Which way to go? *Is a motivating factor a "threat" (e.g., the closing of a local program that will create a big service gap) or an "opportunity" (e.g., the chance to apply for a collaborative grant) for which people may feel a greater sense of urgency to collaborate? Can the team turn a threat into an opportunity for collaboration and systems change?*

Directions: Have the team determine if they can use opportunities and threats identified in their assessment of the community's current context to galvanize the team toward a common purpose. Some teams took advantage of the opportunity to apply for grants for fiscal support in accomplishing team goals as described in Chapter VII. Sometimes even the threat of a potential crisis can be transformed into an opportunity for collaboration as was the case with The South Kingstown, RI, CPP Team.

SOUVENIR

The South Kingstown, RI, CPP Team was faced with the following "threat." When the team was established (2000–01), the South Kingstown School Department had an integrated preschool/kindergarten program known as the South Kingstown Integrated Preschool (SKIP) located at Hazard School. In 2001–02, the district was planning to relocate the kindergartens to their "home elementaries" and move high school classes into Hazard School. The location of the preschool program after 2000–01 was uncertain. In addition, there was no Head Start program in South Kingstown. The only Head Start option was to transport South Kingstown children a long distance to a Head Start program in another community. As a result, few Head Start children attended this out-of-community program despite a waiting list of 20–30 identified Head Start eligible children in South Kingstown. The team used this threat as an impetus to work together to offer blended, collaborative public school preschool/Head Start services in a setting at which additional services for young children and their families were made available.

Fully Engaging a Variety of Stakeholders

Which way to go? *Who should be on the team?*

Directions: Recruit a core team to coordinate the collaborative planning process. The team should include a manageable number of agency and family representatives (as described more fully in the previous chapter). It is critical that team membership include those people who are key to the team successfully addressing its focus. Once the team's focus is determined, the team may need to reexamine its membership and align membership numbers and types with what the team wants to accomplish.

SOUVENIR

The original team consisted of early childhood service providers and parents. We quickly realized that we needed to add people who made decisions that impacted services and families. Elementary school principals were perceived to be not only the "end users" of the early childhood system, but a very powerful influence for the community. Their participation provided much needed momentum to the team's work. We made an all-out effort to get them on board via personal contact. Their joining our core team was a key to our success."

Crowley, LA, Acadia Parish CPP Team

Which way to go? *How can teams ensure that their size is manageable and yet be responsive to a variety of stakeholders?*

Directions: The core team should design an effective multilevel mechanism to promote the full engagement of a variety of stakeholders in a variety of ways that will help the team be successful. In short, buy-in/commitment is not confined to core team members alone. For the plan to translate from paper to practice, buy-in must occur on many levels and include people who must approve and/or fund the plan and people who must implement the plan (e.g., actually implement collaborative policies, participate in collaborative services, complete collaborative forms, etc.). The key is designing stakeholder involvement activities that are meaningful to the planning process and meaningful to the stakeholders themselves.

Some core teams like to do Action Planning themselves, seeking the input of other stakeholders in the planning process through surveys, focus groups, etc. This has the advantage of being more time efficient, particularly in light of people's busy schedules. Other core teams like to use Action Planning teams as a vehicle for greater stakeholder involvement. As described more fully in Chapter VI, they establish time-limited Action Planning teams chaired by core team members with membership including staff and families who are not on the core team. These teams develop action plans to address a particular collaborative priority(ies) and report to the core team. This has the advantage of actively involving more people in plan development. This can be an especially effective way of building the buy-in of direct service staff and families, particularly where they will have some role in plan implementation.

Whether Action Planning is done by the core team or through Action Planning teams composed of core team members and others, the team should establish mechanisms for input from a variety of stakeholders throughout the planning process such as surveys, interviews, focus groups, supplying data/information, and/or reviewing and commenting on plans. Using these mechanisms increases the likelihood that team plans will be relevant to the people impacted by them. It is also a way of informing people about what is going on so they can have a better idea of what to expect from the team's collaboration and making them feel a part of it.

SOUVENIR

"It is important that the team give attention to not only seeking the input of agency leadership, but also involve staff and families. We learned that the more involvement you have, the better your accomplishments. Likewise, the more you accomplish, the more motivated people are to be involved. We surveyed staff and family members to gather information needed to design a resource and referral mechanism that would be responsive to their needs. We also built in training for staff and families to make sure that this new resource would be properly used."

Central Falls, RI, CPP Team

Which way to go? *What is the chain of command within the agencies represented on the team that the team will need to consider in order to get respective agencies' approval for team plans? What is each team member's role in relation to the chain of command of his or her agency? Is he or she a decision-maker? Does he or she have ready* *access to decision-makers, e.g., serving as the decision-makers designee on the team? Are team members administrative staff with some authority over people who may ultimately be asked to implement collaborative team plans? Are they a peer of people who may ultimately implement collaborative team plans? Are there already established channels within the respective agencies that the team can access for information sharing and gathering input of agency staff that will ultimately serve in an approval or implementer role?*

Directions: It is not uncommon for members of a collaborative team to reflect varied levels of decision-making authority relative to the agencies they represent. In addition, decision-making structures vary from agency to agency. Therefore, as part of ground rules development (see Chapter III), articulate how team decisions will be made in light of the respective chains for command of the participating agencies. Establish the expectation that team members will keep key people within their respective agencies (decision-makers and potential implementers) informed about team activities to cultivate buy-in and get people's input throughout the planning process. Few people like a "surprise," no matter how worthy it may be. During these interactions, individual agency decision-makers and potential implementers will likely have suggestions or concerns about team activities. It is better to address these during the planning process so that individual agency decision-makers can then see their issues addressed in the ultimate team recommendations and thus be more likely to support team direction.

Backseat Driving:

Tips on Getting the Support of Key Stakeholders

- Keep stakeholders informed as planning is occurring and before, during, and after decisions are made through memos, e-mails, sharing minutes, newsletters, interviews, staff meetings, parent meetings, etc.;
- Consider any "decisions" of the team as only "recommendations" until adequate input from stakeholders can be obtained;
- Clarify decision-making parameters for the core team in light of the decision-making policies and chains of command of the various agencies; and
- Ensure that stakeholders are actively involved in fine tuning collaborative team plans during implementation as well as in monitoring plan progress and evaluating its impact.

Which way to go? For team members that are parents, are they on the team representing a parent perspective on their own or do they represent a group of parents?

Directions: Many teams find it beneficial to include family representatives on both core and action planning teams. Family members provide the team with "consumer" perspectives. They also offer the team many assets that agency staff may not have, e.g., special skills because of their personal or professional background and/or contacts with community leaders. In some instances, family members can represent the team's "cause" more effectively than staff. It shows agency decision-makers and other public officials that families (their clients and/or voters) are concerned about early childhood—not just professionals.

SOUVENIR The CPP teams involved families in a number of ways. Several had family members on their core team. The co-chair of the South Kingstown, RI, CPP Team was a family member who had no professional connection to early childhood. Some family members wore "two hats"—both professional and parent. Other family members served on the team solely because they were parents. A few teams did not have family members on their core teams but did involve them in other ways, e.g., on action teams, via surveys, and as ad hoc members or presenters.

Which way to go? Who are others in the community whose input or buy-in the team needs but who should not or cannot be regular members of the core team? Do any core team members have effective working relationships with these people?

Directions: On an ad hoc/as needed basis, involve other community members who have a more indirect interest in the team's focus or who have limitations that prevent regular core team membership. This can be done via (1) having them attend periodic meetings at which their interest or area of expertise is discussed or (2) having a core team member solicit their input on relevant issues through personal contact or survey. The following

Collaborative Planning Team Input Form is designed so that it can be filled out during a phone or face-to-face interview and then copied for sharing with the core team.

Collaborative Planning Team Input Form

Name of Person Interviewed: _____

Agency: _____

Address: _____

Phone: _____ **Fax:** _____

E-mail: _____

Team Member Completing This Form: _____

Instructions to Collaborative Team Member Conducting a Phone Call or Meeting to Obtain This Input: Please review the team's focus with the person you are interviewing and have them answer the following questions. Record neatly in a dark color so that clear copies can be made to share with team members.

1. What is your reaction to the focus this team is taking?

2. Which elements of this focus relate to things that you or your organization are doing? What are things we need to know about so that we can coordinate our activities with you?

3. In addition to #2 above, how might the team involve you with what we are doing?

    ____ Include you as a regular member of our team.

    ____ Access your input on a consultative basis (e.g., have you attend a meeting when we discuss particular topics, call you for relevant input, or send you relevant materials for review and comment).

    ____ Include you on our mailing list as an "ex-officio" member to get our meeting minutes.

    ____ Other

4. What other questions or comments do you have?

This form may be reproduced without permission.

SOUVENIR The Westerly, RI, CPP Team used the Collaborative Planning Team Input Form with the following stakeholders related to their goal of linking families of children with special needs to community services: Woman's Health Center at the Westerly Hospital; selected physicians; visiting nurses; Head Start Social Services and Youth Services (Head Start early childhood program was on the CPP team); Parents as Teachers from an adjacent community (Westerly had no Parents as Teachers program prior to CPP); Family Place at the Westerly Library; and Department of Health representatives. Parents as Teachers staff became CPP members who led to the team in successfully applying for a Parents as Teachers grant to address the CPP team goal related to parent outreach. The nurse manager at the Westerly Hospital attended one CPP team meeting as an ad hoc member and helped the CPP team design an agenda for meeting with physicians during rounds. She offered advice on working with physicians and scheduled a meeting for team representatives. The purpose of this meeting was to make them aware of the CPP team and early childhood services and also to ask them to use the Prescription Pad Referral Form (this has had a very positive impact on physician referrals and communications). Physicians gave helpful advice on the Prescription Pad Referral Form for making physician referrals for early intervention or special education (see Chapter IX). Other agencies contacted appreciated being kept "in the loop" and indicated a willingness to be involved on an as needed basis.

Developing Strong Teams Built on Effective People-to-People Relationships

Developing a strong and productive team is the facilitator's ultimate goal. This can be a challenge if the team has not worked together in the past or if it has a rocky history. Even when starting with team members with positive attitudes towards each other, the team will benefit from activities to support effective people-to-people relationships. Through such activities, they will get to know each other better as individuals and as agencies in relation to the collaboration that they are initiating. This will help them build a solid foundation of a collective team identity and evolve

through the various team developmental stages described Chapter II. It is also important to create an environment in which people feel accepted and valued, feel like they can have open discussions without hidden agendas, and feel like problems can be resolved without creating winners and losers.

SOUVENIR "CPP participation showed us the value of mutual respect and support for one another—professional to professional—person to person. Our shared accomplishments are a positive reflection on us all."

South Kingstown, RI, CPP Team

Which way to go? *How can team members get to know each other as individuals?*

Directions: Help team members get acquainted as individuals. Depending on the team's knowledge of each other and their history, the facilitator may find it helpful to have some type of icebreaker or get acquainted activity at the first meeting. There are various ones that can be used. An activity used by some of the CPP teams was "Building a Team Resume." (The directions for this activity appear on the following page.) This activity helps people take off their meeting "masks," interact with each other, and realize the variety of skills and talents in the room among all agency representatives and parents. It's nice to emphasize the varied skills that the team has and how they are stronger collectively than individually.

SOUVENIR "The team resume activity helped us have an 'aha' about the wealth of experience on the team and that no Nevada participants were born within 50 miles of each other!"

Greater Metropolitan Clark County Las Vegas, NV, CPP Team

Activity

Building a Team Resume

1. Assign a facilitator, recorder, and timekeeper. The facilitator, recorder, and timekeeper all participate in this activity along with other team members.

2. The recorder prepares a storyboard (see Chapter III for explanation) by placing five colored header cards across the top of the storyboard to create a matrix, and labeling each card with the following heading titles (it helps to do this prior to the meeting):

   - Yellow: Personal

   - Pink: Professional

   - Green: Education

   - Blue: Volunteer

   - Orange: Current Job Title and Agency of Representation

3. The facilitator reviews with the team these instructions and passes out a packet of cards to each member. Each packet includes a yellow, pink, green, blue, and orange card. Provide a dark marker (any color) for each person.

4. Each team member puts his or her name on each card. Then, he or she completes the cards as follows:

   - Yellow: Personal (Place of birth).

   - Pink: Professional (Number of years person has worked).

   - Green: Education (High school mascot and post-high school education experiences. "School of hard knocks" counts as post-high school education!).

   - Blue: Volunteer (Organizations like Special Olympics or roles such as church organist).

   - Orange: Current Job Title and Agency or Representation (List as applicable).

5. Each team member places his or her cards under the appropriate header column on the storyboard.

6. The facilitator asks team members to come up and review what has been posted on the storyboard. He or she helps the team note similarities and differences among members.

7. At the conclusion of the activity, the facilitator asks team members to share:

   - Observations about their team based on this activity, and

   - Attributes that the team can use to help the collaborative planning process.

8. The timekeeper helps the team keep track of time, allowing a total of 30 minutes for this activity (vary time depending on size of the team).

This activity may be reproduced without permission.

Backseat Driving:

Tips for Relationship Building

Getting acquainted is not a one-time event. The team should be attuned to helping team members get better acquainted over time, building positive working relationships. Teams should be alert for the following:

1. Pay attention to team cohesion related to some members perhaps feeling "on the inside" and others "on the outside" and intervene as appropriate, e.g., striking up conversations with those "on the outside" and trying to find them a way to be more involved.

2. Be prepared to start every meeting with introductions in case new people or ad hoc members attend.

3. Have periodic times for socialization. Some teams lunched together prior to starting their meetings. Morning meetings lend themselves to "coffee time" prior to the meeting for connecting. One team had an informal gathering with refreshments one evening to celebrate and reflect on accomplishments.

4. Have a process to orient new members as they are added to the team. For example, identify a team member to orient each new member and to be that person's "buddy" during the first year on the team. Provide a notebook or file of team orientation materials.

Which way to go? *How can team members get to know each other as agencies?*

Directions: Help team members also get acquainted as agencies. This task can be done by having agency representatives fill out an Agency Profile (provided in this chapter) and sharing it along with agency brochures and related information at the first or second meeting. This activity provides team members with practical information that they find useful and helps establish a collective community awareness that sets the scene for conducting the assessment of the current community context and initiating planning. CPP staff facilitators discovered that every team benefited from this activity. Without exception, team members learned new things about resources in their own communities, even among agencies with which they regularly collaborated. Team members valued this information so much that most teams ended up developing service directories of various types to be available for staff and/or families. In some instances, as agency profiles were shared, members spontaneously started networking and talking about opportunities to collaborate.

SOUVENIR

"All of us have more information about each other's agencies. Our work is still mostly internal. The collaboration has helped in writing grants to improve accountability and community participation for different agencies and organizations. Specifically, Bright Beginnings (welcome wagon) has added contact information for early childhood services and Child Find to their welcome packets given to all new families. Bright Beginnings is planting seeds for future positive feelings about early intervention."

Longmont, CO, St. Vrain Early Childhood CPP Team

Agency Profile

Instructions: Provide information on services relevant to the education and care of young children, including children with and without disabilities. Keep responses brief—a basic, reader-friendly description of what you do. If you have multiple resources/programs, complete this profile for each, copying this form as needed.

Purpose: To learn what services we have in our community to help us:
  (1) get to know each other, and
  (2) have information to use in our planning.

Agency/Program Name: _____

Population eligible (age, income, special needs, etc.) _____
_____

Services _____

Number of children enrolled _____

Service hours _____

Service location(s) _____

Funding mechanism(s) _____

How families access services _____
_____

Parent fees, if any _____

Potential collaboration topics _____
_____

Contact person _____

Other comments _____

_____

_____

_____

This form may be reproduced without permission.

Which way to go? *Do team members have a positive history of working together individually or collectively? If positive, how can this history be related to this new collaboration?*

Directions: If the team has a positive history, plan an activity for them to reflect on their previous endeavors and learnings from these activities that can serve as a foundation for this new collaboration (building success on success).

Which way to go? *Do team members have a negative history of working together individually or collectively? Who were the involved parties? What happened? What evidence exists, if any, that a negative impact is still being felt? That is, is it in the past or is this past still affecting the way that people interact with each other? How is this manifesting itself? What were the root causes of this negativity and how can they be addressed in a way to create a more positive climate for collaboration?*

Directions: If the team has a negative history, consider whether or not this past should be discussed openly with this team. If it does emerge, intentionally or not, the team should reflect on the key factors that led to negative results (in a nonaccusatory, objective way) and learnings from this experience to increase the likelihood that this new collaboration will be positive.

SOUVENIR

The Cranston, RI, CPP Team learned the benefit of airing previous problems and using these as learnings rather than seeing them as obstacles for collaboration. They had had some problems in the past related to transition. In fact, because of these problems, the team targeted transition as one of its primary focuses. As they began planning, old problems emerged. They took time during one of their meetings to "get these out in the open." Rather than perseverating on these problems or allowing these issues to remain "hidden agendas," they turned them into learnings and refocused the discussion on an identification of issues to keep in mind as the team worked on its plan for improving transition.

SOUVENIR

"We learned the importance of forgetting the past and moving on and of people being willing to forgive and forget past troubles and move forward together in a collaborative manner. Members of the planning team were willing to come together and try to renew troubled relationships. Ground rules made the meetings a 'safe' place where they could openly discuss difficult issues. One of our ground rules was 'no agency bashing.' We realized that we shared a common vision and that everyone wanted to improve the quality of services for young children and their families. When times got tough during the course of the year, team members could always renew momentum by remembering the shared purpose and why we were meeting in the first place."

Denver, CO, CPP Team

Which way to go? *What are strategies for promoting harmonious team interactions?*

Directions: Have the team identify their criteria for effective team work, addressing the way they will interact as part of ground rules development. Suggestions in the sample ground rules provided in Chapter III related to interactions are:

- Be realistic; respect others' right to say no.

- Share ideas and air time.

- All ideas have value . . . even ones with which we disagree.

- Honor confidentiality related to children, families, team members, and agencies. Adopt the rule "what you say here, stays here."

The facilitator can support the team in developing active listening skills by having the team practice these skills and by facilitator modeling on an ongoing basis. As mentioned in Chapter III, have the team conclude each meeting by reflecting not only what it accomplished but also how the members worked together as a team.

Backseat Driving:

Tips on Working With People

- People skills are key to effective collaboration.
- People like to be treated with respect and to be able to trust and be trusted.
- People like recognition and good news. Give each other positive feedback.
- People want to be understood. Seek to understand their programs and issues.
- People will be *less* likely to change a position if they are forced to defend it.

Which way to go? *What are tools for conflict resolution?*

Directions: Promote win-win solutions, focusing on issues and not positions. A position presents only one way in which a problem can be resolved, e.g., "We think this child should be placed in this particular setting with this particular teacher." An issue-oriented approach identifies key characteristics of what the team is trying to achieve, giving room within which to negotiate, e.g., "We think that this child should receive services in a setting that has these characteristics . . ." Win-win solutions address legitimate interests of all members to the extent possible in a way that resolves conflict fairly, that takes common interests into consideration, and that is durable (Fisher and Ury, 1981). If a team member articulates a position, don't attack. Seek to understand. Ask clarifying questions to identify underlying issues needing to be addressed. Then have the team brainstorm a variety of possible solutions to address those issues, the merit of which can each be evaluated. Or, depending on the nature of preceding team discussion, show how issues raised by this particular team member relate to the issues of others or team direction. In short, try to refocus them from 'me' to 'we.'

Team activities involving problem solving and brainstorming are productive exercises but also run the risk of being opportunities for conflicts and blaming. Members may become polarized, competitive, and confrontational with less concern for team relationships and more concern for personal or agency-specific needs. As a result of these interchanges, a "pecking order" may emerge. To some degree, this is an natural evolution of team leadership. However, the facilitator should also seek to nominalize the group as much as possible so that all members feel they have equal value on the team even though their respective agency roles or authority may not be the same. Throughout team interchanges, it is critical that the facilitator honor all members and show no favoritism to one over another.

Are We There Yet?

Advice on helping teams evaluate their progress and evolve to the next stage.

The team should ask itself the following questions:

1. Does the team include the right people needed to get the job done? Are they involved in ways that are meaningful to them and to the team's overall focus?

2. Do members appear committed to the direction the team is taking?

3. Do all core team members have something important to contribute at most meetings, e.g., a report or a meeting task? In short, do they have a reason to come to the meeting? Is the workload evenly distributed?

4. Do people get along? Are they working together harmoniously and in a win-win way? Are people treating each other as equals and valued partners? Are there cliques? Does the team operate as a cohesive unit?

5. Does the team have ground rules for team interactions, ongoing communications with decision-makers and other stakeholders, involvement with others in the community, and orientation of new members? Are these ground rules being followed? Are they producing desired results?

Chapter V

Determining the Destination

Establishing a Shared Vision

The activities outlined in each of the chapters in this manual are not isolated events. Rather, they are all interrelated, one activity building on another. For example, activities outlined in previous chapters are designed to help the team get organized by having members become familiar with each other, assessing the community's current context related to early childhood services, identifying an initial team focus, establishing ground rules, and developing stakeholder relationships and involvement. These activities lay the groundwork for the team being able to turn its attention to where it wants to go on its journey of collaboration—its shared vision.

SOUVENIR "Developing a shared vision helps to unify the team, providing the big picture (thinking big) from which smaller and more attainable goals can be established."

Central Falls, RI, CPP Team

The team's vision is the "destination" the team wants to reach as a result of its journey of collaboration. It is the statement that binds the team in traveling in a common direction, creating "a sense of commonality that permeates" the team "and gives coherence to diverse activities" in which the team engages over time (Senge, 1990, p. 206). The vision:

1. Describes the community context that the team would like to create at some point in the future (usually three to five years);

2. Builds on the past and present community context but does not simply extend it (not just more of the same);

3. Is concrete and reasonably attainable, including doing some new things and taking some risks; and

4. Is uplifting, compelling people to action.

In the early stages, the team does not have a "track record." Team members may question or lack confidence in what the team can actually achieve. Therefore, it may be more feasible to start with a narrow vision that is more easily achievable. If successful, team members will gain confidence in the team's ability to work together and will, thus, be able to envision more comprehensive possibilities for team efforts. In effect, a true vision is likely to emerge over time as team members get to know each other, accomplish meaningful things together, and thereby, come to appreciate their own true potential to address complex community issues. Fullan (1993) speaks to this issue, echoing Senge (1990) when he explains:

> First, under conditions of dynamic complexity one needs a good deal of reflective experience before one can form a plausible vision. Vision emerges from, more than it precedes, action. Even then it is always provisional. Second, shared vision, which is essential for success, must evolve through the dynamic interaction of organizational members and leaders. This takes time and will not succeed unless the vision-building process is somewhat open-ended. Visions coming later does not mean that they are not worked on. Just the opposite. They are pursued more authentically while avoiding premature formalization. (p. 28)

SOUVENIR

"The vision and goals of the planning group need to be perceived as highly important for each member in attendance."

*Greater Metropolitan Clark County
Las Vegas, NV, CPP Team*

The vision should be more than a "piece of paper." To make the vision a reality, it will require the involvement and buy-in of both core team members and also staff and families of the agencies they represent. It is important that this vision be shared among various stakeholders in the agencies represented on the team (Senge, 1990). Thus, vision development should include input of not only the core team but also the stakeholders they represent (see Chapter IV).

This chapter addresses:

1. Developing a shared team vision meaningful to all team members, and

2. Extending the vision beyond the team to key community stakeholders and keeping it alive over time.

Developing a Shared Team Vision Meaningful to All Team Members

Which way to go? *How can the team ensure that the vision is "real" for team members? What strategies help team members buy into the vision and actively work toward its achievement? How can the team ensure that the vision meets both individual agency and community needs?*

Directions: Anchor the vision in the current context of individual agencies (as revealed through the sharing of agency profiles) and the community (as revealed through the assessment of the current community context) as discussed in Chapters III and IV. These activities help team members develop a common understanding of each other and the community "system." It gets them "on the same page." Areas of common ground generally become apparent. This common ground becomes the foundation for making visioning and subsequent planning more concrete and relevant to day-to-day agency needs. The more that plans build on and relate to the needs of individual agencies as well as the community at large, the greater the likelihood that meaningful change will continue when planning ends and plan implementation begins (Rous, Hemmeter, & Schuster, 1999; Guskey & Huberman, 1995; Fullan, 1993). In short, anchoring the vision in the current context will help team members feel like team activities will benefit them individually and they will be more likely to buy in and work toward the team vision.

Backseat Driving:

Tips for Making the Vision Real

Project staff found that some team members had previously engaged in visioning in other settings. Often, these visions were not meaningful to members or there was never any real follow-through. As a result, even the term *visioning* put some team members off. To offset potential skepticism:

- Team members generally include both concrete and abstract thinkers. Visioning is essentially an abstract activity. Accommodate both team member styles by anchoring the vision in the current context of individual agencies and the community to make visioning more concrete. Anchoring also helps make the vision more relevant.

- Clarify that the vision articulates team direction for moving from the current context to what the team hopes to accomplish.

- Target the vision's broad or narrow scope depending on the developmental stage and interests of the team (e.g., Is it a newly forming team? A high performing team with a long history? A team where you have trouble getting everyone to the table?).

- Start with a vision that is concrete and reasonably attainable. As the team progresses, it can revise and expand its vision.

- Build team capacity to do future thinking and to be proactive. Help them realize this by facilitating discussions such as those suggested here through which they reach this conclusion on their own—rather than having the facilitator preach to them.

- Don't worry about having an eloquent vision statement. Rather than spending time on "wordsmithing," make sure the vision wording communicates to team members and relevant stakeholders and then move on to addressing challenges to the vision through action planning. Accomplishments resulting from these actions will help the vision have deeper meaning and evolve over time.

Which way to go? *What if team members have trouble thinking beyond the day-to-day and thus consider it meaningless to think about the future? What if they see their problems as beyond their control? What if they are preoccupied with doing only that which they are required legally to do?*

Directions: An impediment to visioning is often the difficulty that some people have with future thinking or believing that they can actually impact their own problems. The facilitator may hear remarks such as, "there is nothing we can do." Another phenomenon in this age of mandates is that the facilitator may hear reluctance to go beyond minimal requirements with comments like, "is it in the law?" or "just tell me what I have to do." Such remarks indicate a "victim or reactive mentality" to changes forced on them rather than consideration of proactive changes that team members would actually like to see. These individuals may think it is pointless to plan, because they do not feel they are in control of their current context. If they are perseverating on problems over which they feel they have no control or if they seem unwilling to do future thinking, the facilitator can help by having them:

- Answer the question, "how would you like for this current situation to look differently (the vision) whether or not we can fully impact these issues immediately?" (then, when the team does Action Planning, the team can brainstorm options over which they have some control that would be steps toward making that vision a reality);

- Think of one or two problems in the past that they were able to successfully overcome (on an interagency basis if possible, but if not, on an individual agency basis) and learnings from solving those problems that would offer guidance for creating change in this new situation;

- Brainstorm the various ways in which they can choose to respond to mandates beyond their control, emphasizing that the team may not be able to control what they are required to do, but they do have some control over how they respond;

- Challenge the team to think in new ways and take positive risks;

- Discuss and sort issues into those over which the team has (1) much control, (2) some control, and (3) no control, focusing attention on issues over which the team has much or some control; and/or

- Focus attention on those issues most common to the needs of all team members in hopes that the majority of members will buy into creating a vision to address those needs, thereby creating a "critical mass" of support on the team that more pessimistic members may agree to support, even if with some initial reservations.

Then, hopefully, early team successes in moving toward the vision—even small victories—will help build the confidence of pessimistic members.

SOUVENIR

"A vision helps the team focus its efforts. Developing a vision aided in building the 'trust factor,' helping the team establish common ground and a reason to work together in a way that would meet both individual and collective needs."

Cranston, RI, CPP Team

Which way to go? *What is an activity that will fully involve all team members in vision formulation?*

Directions: Use an activity for visioning that actively involves all members such as the visioning activity provided here. The resulting statement can take several forms as depicted by the accompanying souvenirs.

Activity

Visioning Activity

Focus Question: Related to our chosen area(s) of team focus, what is the community context you want our team to create in three to five years? What concrete and doable procedures and/or services do you want to see in place? How are children and families benefiting?

1. Appoint a facilitator, recorder, and timekeeper.

2. The **recorder** sets up a storyboard with a heading of "Our Vision." The focus question is written on flip chart paper and posted near the storyboard.

3. **Each team member** identifies 3-5 answers to the focus questions, recording one answer per 4" x 6" sticky note* with a marker.

4. **Each team member** posts all sticky notes on chart.

5. The **facilitator** presents the focus question to the team and leads them in merging similar ideas into vertical columns headed by a blank sticky note (heading).

6. The **recorder** notes the name/title of each column on the heading sticky note. These names/titles become the characteristics describing the vision the team wants to create.

7. The **timekeeper** helps the team track time (25 minutes).

* This activity calls for sticky notes. It can also be done using a storyboard with note cards as described in Chapter III, "Backseat Driving: Tips for Using a Storyboard."

This activity may be reproduced without permission.

Westerly, RI, Team Vision—

Who are we and what is our focus: As a collaborative team of parents and professionals representing early intervention, child care, Head Start, and public schools, we are committed to increasing the involvement of parents in the education and care of their children ages birth to six with and without disabilities with emphasis related to the needs of unidentified, unserved, and underserved children who have developmental delays and behavioral challenges.

What is our vision for what we want to see in our community in three to five years to benefit children and families: Appropriate supports in our community make it possible for parents of children ages birth to six with typical and atypical development (1) to know about typical and atypical child development and developmentally appropriate practice in order to work with their children and to recognize quality programs, and (2) to know what help is available and how to access it.

What services and supports do we hope to put in place to make this vision a reality:

1. A mechanism through which all families of newborns will be introduced to "the system," e.g., a gift bag with community resources information, developmental checklist, etc.

2. A resource directory that tells parents how to access services. The directory would be widely available, e.g., in gift bags, doctors' offices, community agencies, libraries, toy stores, clothing stores, hospitals, Realtors, church and synagogue leaders, etc.

3. Resource materials associated with topics in the vision in various formats (e.g., print, video) for parents that could be included in the gift bag, used as part of training and support groups, etc.

4. Parenting classes and support groups that cover topics such as typical and atypical development and how to access needed services. Classes and support groups build on existing programs and are offered through a variety of ways and schedules to meet varied needs of families, e.g., typically unserved and underserved populations, working parents who cannot attend programs on weekdays, at-home moms and dads (perhaps a Moms' Club and/or hands-on activities, e.g., field trips beneficial to both child and parent).

5. Increased physician communication with early childhood programs.

6. A Birth to Six Early Childhood Center that is a site for (1) direct service programs (e.g., Early Intervention, child care, Head Start, public school),

(2) parent training classes, (3) parent support groups, (4) family oriented programs such as free magic shows, family nights, gymborees, etc., (5) resource materials (centralized resource area in the community), and (6) a single point of contact for families.

7. A network of agencies, doctors, and providers who (1) all give parents the same message, (2) communicate with each other, (3) link with each other to coordinate services and provide support to each other, and (4) see themselves as a network of varied resources/options to meet the varied needs of children and families.

The Denver, CO, CPP Team Vision— "Service Coordination for infants and toddlers is competent, available, well informed, and consistent."

Vision for St. Vrain Early Childhood Council CPP Team, Longmont, CO—"In three years, we want to see enough staff to support the early childhood needs of all young children and their families (ages birth through five) in the St. Vrain community and sufficient bilingual professionals to meet the needs of mono-lingual preschool community members provided by early childhood agencies. Immediate goals toward that vision—develop a collaborative system to ensure (1) the availability and accessibility for early identification of children with special needs or who are at risk for future developmental concerns and (2) family supports."

Extending the Vision Beyond the Team to Key Community Stakeholders and Keeping It Alive Over Time

Which way to go? *Can you change the vision?*

Directions: A vision is not written in stone. As mentioned earlier, teams may choose to start with a more narrow vision and then, after they have some successes together, expand it to address the early childhood service system more comprehensively. As progress is made toward the vision, the vision begins to "take life" and has more meaning for people. The picture of what is possible truly comes into focus. At such a point, the team may choose to refine the original vision to be more in keeping with team learnings along the way or to add greater specificity to the vision. Finally, as the vision becomes a reality, the team may choose to develop a new vision, extending it further into the future to address additional unmet needs.

SOUVENIR

"The vision is an evolutionary thing. It starts out as words on paper. As you make progress toward your vision, it begins to become more real. As you progress, the team should revisit and fine-tune to make it more concrete and in keeping with team members' evolving perspectives. Time spent in developing the vision is very important, because it gives the team a focus. You can't touch lightly on this activity."

South Kingstown, RI, CPP Team

Which way to go? *How can the team build support for the vision in the community beyond core team members?*

Directions: The team will increase the likelihood that the vision will become a reality if it builds support for the vision beyond team members. Tasks and tools for building support among leaders, line staff, and families of the agencies represented on the core team are described in this chapter and more fully in Chapter IV. One method is through public awareness. Another method is targeting specific people or groups who are key to the vision becoming a reality, e.g., physicians, families in the community, the local school board. The South Kingstown, RI, souvenir related to the team's relationship development with the local school board (School Committee) provides many valuable lessons.

SOUVENIR

Teams promoted awareness of early childhood, their teams, and their vision or priority issues through various means:

- **Child Find Public Awareness**—Acadia Parish, Crowley, LA; Central Falls, RI; Metropolitan Clark County, Las Vegas, NV; South Kingstown, RI; St. Vrain Early Childhood Council, CO
- **Publishing community early childhood services directories**—Acadia Parish, Crowley, LA; Central Falls, RI; Cranston, RI; South Kingstown, RI
- **Working with Physicians**—Westerly, RI
- **Participation in Public Events**—Acadia Parish, Crowley, LA, Literacy Walk; Early childhood booth at Westerly, RI, school district community fair
- **Community Early Childhood Newsletter** published by the team—Part of the plan to be implemented in South Kingstown, RI
- **Use of the media**—Interviews on the radio regarding child development and tips for parents in Westerly, RI; newspaper articles in South Kingstown, RI, and Westerly, RI

SOUVENIR

The South Kingstown, RI, CPP Team established ongoing dialogue with the School Committee (the local board of education) to help cultivate a truly "shared vision" with this group of key stakeholders. The team's vision was to establish a comprehensive, inclusive, collaborative birth–five early childhood service center for ALL children with and without special needs with related supports for families such as comprehensive parenting programs, resource materials, etc. They concluded that building a commitment from the School Committee to this vision would be a process that would take place not in a single meeting but over time. Team members were careful in their interactions with the School Committee to (1) build positive relationships based on common goals, (2) establish the team's credibility as an effective group, (3) educate the School Committee about early childhood and collaboration, (4) express gratitude for both conceptual and tangible support, and (5) be patient and satisfied with incremental progress. "Our attitude of gratitude was received well by a School Committee that usually just hears criticism."

1. First meeting with School Committee in April, 2000:

- Met to familiarize them with the CPP team, the vision, and community needs such as the uncertain future of the Hazard School (former integrated preschool/kindergarten center—kindergartens were being moved to their home elementaries), the lack of Head Start services in the community, the fragmentation of services for young children, and the need for more family support programs. Emphasized the consistency of the CPP team's goals with the district's strategic plan related to early childhood. In short, the CPP team offered themselves as a vehicle for achieving district goals.

- Invited RI Department of Education preschool special education coordinator to present on state initiatives and how South Kingstown's efforts related to inclusion, NAEYC accreditation, and initiating this collaborative team were considered exemplary.

- Asked CPP facilitator to present on national trends and the efficacy of early childhood services and collaboration.

- Did **not** ask the School Committee for anything except advice on team direction. The School Committee was impressed with this, noting that it was a rare for a group to present to them without demands. They were also impressed with the team's makeup reflecting broad interagency support and parent/professional partnerships. Several School Committee members expressed strong support for early childhood services.

2. Meeting with School Committee in November, 2000:

- Provided update on the team's several accomplishments that were achieved through collaboration of existing resources (rather than infusion of new funds).

- Received School Committee support "in concept" for CPP team direction. Some School Committee members asked to be kept informed and invited to CPP meetings.

- As an outgrowth of this meeting, CPP team members met with the superintendent to develop a budget proposal for the coming year. Ultimately, a major outcome was co-location of a variety of services (inclusive preschool services, Head Start preschool class and parent training program, early intervention, Parents as Teachers, Child Outreach/Child Find) in a public school facility at the Hazard School along with a second Head Start class at another elementary school with no infusion of new resources beyond those that were readily available to member agencies for their own programs.

3. Meeting with School Committee in November, 2001:

- Provided update on the team's continuing accomplishments, including data on benefits to children and families.

- Thanked School Committee for their ongoing support of CPP team efforts.

- An outcome of this meeting was the team working with the superintendent to develop a budget request for continued and expanded use of Hazard School as a comprehensive, interagency, blended, inclusive early childhood center and for a new position of Early Childhood Coordinator for the 2002–03 budget (position previously nonexistent).

Which way to go? *How do you keep the vision alive over time?*

Directions: Teams can keep the vision alive by regularly reviewing it to remind team members of their reason for existence. As new members join the team, it is important that they buy into the vision. Therefore, time should be set aside on a meeting agenda for reviewing the vision, allowing the opportunity for vision refinement to ensure that it is relevant to all members, both new and old. Teams can also keep the vision alive by keeping it relevant. It is helpful to periodically evaluate the vision, e.g., annually or after reaching major accomplishments or roadblocks toward its accomplishment. If the vision is truly grounded in the needs of individual team members/agencies and their priorities, it will live on even if the nature of the team changes as exemplified by the following Acadia Parish, LA, souvenir.

SOUVENIR

The Acadia Parish CPP Team, Crowley, LA, established the following vision—"In three years, there will be . . . (highest priority):

- Someone named to coordinate all available services for children, birth through kindergarten.
- A comprehensive developmentally appropriate early childhood program that meets the needs of all children.
- Mentors for families: one-to-one support.

In the future, there will also be . . . (lesser priority):

- Access to available resources at school level for Pre-K, kindergarten teachers.
- Increased availability of transportation for families and children.
- Additional Pre-K classes for all lower elementary school and Head Start.
- Meaningful inclusion with peers for all children, birth through kindergarten.
- Increased funding for Human Resources."

This vision still resonates with team members even though the CPP team is not currently meeting in its previous form. Having accomplished the development and distribution of a service directory to staff and families as a CPP team, CPP team members are now continuing the work started on the CPP team via participation on the community's Pre-K team that is working to develop a consistent curriculum for all young children in the parish. This team also conducted a collaborative inservice on curriculum for children attending Even Start, Head Start, and public and private preschools in the area so that children can all start out on the "same page." Head Start and Even Start continue to work together closely since CPP. Head Start, Pre-K, Even Start, and public schools collaborated on a "Literacy Walk," a public awareness campaign on the importance of reading. Each family participating received a free book.

Backseat Driving:

Tips on Keeping the Vision Alive

- Start each meeting with a review of the vision. To build team ownership, at each meeting have a different team member read or summarize the vision or parts of the vision.
- Keep the vision visible by recording it on a flip chart that is posted at each meeting or affixing the vision to the cover of the team's notebook or folder.
- Periodically review and, if needed, refine the vision to keep it relevant, e.g., (1) annually, (2) when new members join the team, or (3) after reaching major accomplishments or roadblocks.

Are We There Yet?

Advice on helping teams evaluate their progress and evolve to the next stage.

The team should ask itself the following questions:

1. Is the vision grounded in the current context of individual agency and community needs? Does it describe the community context the team would like to create at some point in the future (usually three to five years)? Is it concrete and reasonably attainable, including doing some new things and taking some risks? Is it uplifting, compelling people to action?

2. Can all team members summarize the vision and tell why the vision is important to them?

3. How does/has the team shared its vision with other key stakeholders in their respective agencies and with other people or groups in the community who are key to the vision becoming a reality? To what extent do these individuals share the team's vision?

Chapter VI

Mapping the Journey
Setting Priorities and Action Planning

The vision is articulated as the team's desired "destination" for three to five years in the future. Once the vision is in place, the team can then assess gaps between the current community context and the vision. These gaps are challenges the team will need to address so that their vision will ultimately become a reality. It is unlikely that the team will be able to address all of the challenges immediately or at the same time due to the time demands of their own jobs as well as team activities. Fullan (1991, 1993) advises thinking big and starting small with identified priorities for change. That is, the core team should determine the priority challenges to this vision and a time period for which they want to develop action plans (typically one year) in order to take steps toward the vision three to five years in the future. Priority challenges evolve into objectives for the team's action plan, which is the "roadmap" outlining the various legs of its journey of collaboration. This roadmap clearly articulates plans for overcoming roadblocks or challenges standing in the way of where the team is now and where they want to go. This chapter addresses supporting the team in translating the vision from paper into reality, including:

- Setting priorities, and

- Action Planning.

SOUVENIR

Team reflections about thinking big and starting small:

- **Acadia Parish, Crowley, LA**—"The first versions of our vision were all-encompassing and broad based. They were noble but overwhelming. The team prioritized and decided to focus on a project we could do together that would have the biggest impact on young children and families."

- **Cranston, RI**—"It is important to set priorities, selecting those that are doable. 'Thinking big but starting small' results in tasks that, when achieved, help the team bond. These bonds serve as the foundation for continued collaborations."

- **Greater Metropolitan Clark County, Las Vegas, NV**—"The rapid population growth in Las Vegas has impacted each agency on the team. There are not enough resources to provide quality services for new families moving to the area. In this kind of crisis mode and constant change, it's harder to work on comprehensive systems change. We responded by narrowing and prioritizing our vision into a manageable task of increasing public awareness."

- **St. Vrain Early Childhood Council, Longmont, CO—** "We dreamed big dreams while creating our original vision. It was inspiring and overwhelming at the same time. Based upon this, we listed 20 different goals. When the time came to write specific strategies for each of the goals, we realized the reality of available time and energy and *reprioritized* accordingly."

Setting Priorities

Which way to go? *What criteria will the team use for priority setting?*

Directions: Teams often have difficulty setting priorities, because many, if not all, ideas seem important. Certainly, the ideas are important to the team members who generated them. The issue becomes which of these important ideas will the team pursue and in what sequence. It is helpful in making such decisions to consider many factors or criteria for prioritizing challenges. The priority setting criteria should be clear, objective, and mutually acceptable to all members. Such criteria is helpful not only for identifying priority challenges. It is also useful in building the team's capacity to make thoughtful and wise decisions based on multiple factors—more than something just sounding like a good idea. Effective decision-making skills will be valuable throughout the team's work—in deciding on strategies to pursue, in evaluating the effectiveness of team efforts, and so on.

It is helpful to start with some examples of criteria such as those suggested in the following "Backseat Driving: Tips for Criteria for Setting Priorities" to give the team some ideas on which they can build to develop their own criteria of factors important to them.

Backseat Driving:

Tips for Criteria for Setting Priorities

The following are factors for teams to consider in establishing criteria for priority setting. The issue under consideration:

- Is one on which there is the most agreement among team members.
- Relates to individual and community needs.
- Is doable within limited time frame.
- Is most urgent due to legal, funding, or local considerations.
- Requires the least time and funds to implement.
- Provides high and positive visibility and PR for team and participating agencies so that member agencies feel good about this team.
- Is least disruptive to current practice—thereby more easily accepted, creating greater openness to subsequent changes.
- Is likely to result in a quick and public victory to establish a foundation of success and provide momentum for further team activities.

Which way to go? *What are priority challenges that reflect gaps between the community's current context and the vision the team would like to create? How can these be identified in a way that seems fair to all? What if team members have trouble agreeing on priorities?*

Directions: Challenges may be readily apparent as a result of applying the team's decision-making criteria in light of its assessment of the community's current context (SWOTs) and visioning. As a result, the facilitator may be able to help the team target priority challenges and the sequence in which these are to be approached simply through discussion. If consensus cannot be reached on challenges to pursue, the team will need to conduct an activity for this purpose (such as the following one) or use strategies such as those identified in "Backseat Driving: Tips for When the Team Cannot Readily Decide on Priority Challenges" that appears later in this chapter.

Activity

Activity to Identify Priority Challenges the Team Will Address Via Action Planning

Focus Question: Given our SWOTs (our current context), our vision, and our criteria for decision-making, what are challenges we will need to address via one year action plans so that our long-term vision can be achieved?

1. Appoint a facilitator, recorder, and timekeeper.

2. The **recorder** sets up a storyboard with a heading of "Team Challenges." The focus question is written on flip chart paper and posted beside the storyboard.

3. The **facilitator** presents the focus question and **each team member** identifies 2–4 answers to the focus question, recording one answer per 4" x 6" sticky note* with a marker.

4. **Each team member** posts all sticky notes on chart.

5. The **facilitator** rereads the focus question to the team and leads them in merging similar ideas into groups, arranging sticky notes in vertical columns with a blank sticky note at the top of the column.

6. The **recorder** notes the primary theme or concept of each column on the blank sticky note at the top of the column. These themes become the challenges that the team will consider pursuing.

7. The **facilitator** leads the team in deciding which grouping(s) to pursue, using modified consensus. That is, what are challenges that the team can live with and publicly support? The team may decide to start with only one challenge, noting other challenges for future reference. When the initial challenge is addressed, they can reconsider other challenges. They may also choose more than one challenge or all challenges. Teams are encouraged to "think big and start small," choosing challenges to address that are both beneficial and doable in a reasonable amount of time with a little or no additional resources beyond those readily available through participating agencies.

8. The **timekeeper** helps the team track time (30 minutes).

* This activity calls for sticky notes. It can also be done using a storyboard with note cards as described in Chapter III, "Backseat Driving: Tips for Using a Storyboard."

This activity may be reproduced without permission.

Backseat Driving:

Tips for When the Team Cannot Readily Decide on Priority Challenges

If the team cannot decide on priority challenges via discussion as part of the activity outlined in this chapter, another method is needed. Voting for and against is discouraged, because it creates winners and losers, something that will undermine a spirit of collaboration. Rather, options for the facilitator are to have the team review its decision-making criteria and:

- Use modified consensus (see sample ground rules in Chapter III). If team members cannot live with and publicly support priority challenges as listed, ask them to identify what they would (1) add, (2) delete, or (3) change so that they could. From this, the team should be able to identify at least one challenge to get them started.

- Ask if there are any groupings of challenges for which members have objections. Then, focus attention only on those challenges for which there are "no objections."

- Give each member red, yellow, and green dots. Red = Stop, we should not pursue now. Yellow = Caution, this challenge has some merit, but I have concerns about it. Green = Go, this would be a worthwhile challenge to pursue now. Then, discuss and make decisions on those groupings that have only green dots. If there are no such groupings, select the groupings with the most green and fewest yellow dots. Discuss the sources of concern and see if these can be adequately addressed in some way so that pursing this challenge is something with which team members can live.

- Tell team members to rank challenges by putting three dots on their first choice, two dots on their second choice, and one dot on their third choice. They cannot put all of their dots on one choice. Dots must be placed on three separate challenges as instructed. Then, total the dots so that the team can determine the ranking: first priority (most dots), second, third, etc. This may assist the team not only in deciding which challenge to pursue, but also the sequence in which the team would prefer addressing each challenge.

Which way to go? *Which challenges should the team tackle first? How many challenges should the team try to address in its initial activities?*

Directions: There are an infinite number of areas around which collaboration could occur. Each agency will likely have its own issues on which it would like the team to focus. Moreover, there may be various funding and time constraints impacting the ability of people to be involved in collaborative activities. With these factors in mind, start with the priority challenges on which there is most agreement, limiting the number and scope of priorities to those that are doable within a reasonable amount of time with a little or no additional resources beyond those readily available through participating agencies. In short, "think big and start small."

SOUVENIR

Some teams started with only one major priority for initial activities:

- **Acadia Parish, Crowley, LA—Service directory.**
- **Central Falls, RI—Service directory and single point of access.**
- **Greater Metropolitan Clark County, Las Vegas, NV—Child Find Public Awareness.**

Some teams worked on multiple priorities one at a time.

- **Cranston, RI—Focused first on establishing the Cranston Cabinet and then addressed development of a universal release of information form.**

SOUVENIR

Denver, St. Vrain, South Kingstown, and Westerly teams worked on multiple priorities all at the same time. The Westerly, RI, CPP Team identified seven (7) major objectives, articulating the way in which they would like to overcome the challenges in order to put their vision in place. (See a copy of their vision in Chapter V.) They projected staggering implementation of these objectives over a multiyear time frame rather than being overwhelmed by trying to do everything at once. To see where they were as of November 2002, see Chapter IX.

Westerly, RI, CPP Team

Objectives (numbers do not reflect priority order)	Short Term— Spring 2000	Next Year— 2000–2001	Long Term— 2001–2003
1. A mechanism through which all families of newborns (names provided by Health Department) will be introduced to the system, e.g., a "welcome" wagon type of gift bag with community resources information, developmental checklist, etc.	Develop action plan and initiate implementation.	Implement action plan. Evaluate action plan/mechanism.	Refine action plan/mechanism and continue implementation as long as mechanism is having a positive impact.
2. A resource directory that tells parents how to access services. The directory would be widely available, e.g., in the gift bags, doctors' offices, community agencies, libraries, toy stores, clothing stores, hospitals, through Realtors, via church and synagogue leaders, etc.	Develop action plan and initiate implementation.	Implement action plan. Evaluate action plan/directory.	Refine action plan/directory and continue implementation as long as directory is having a positive impact.
3. An increase in physician communication with early childhood programs.	Develop action plan and initiate implementation.	Implement action plan. Evaluate action plan.	Refine action plan; continue to implement as long as strategies are having a positive impact.
4. A network of agencies, doctors, and providers who (a) all give parents the same message, (b) communicate with each other, (c) link with each other to coordinate services and support each other, and (d) see themselves as a network of varied resources/ options regarding varied needs of children/ families.	By June 2000, establish an ongoing interagency structure/network for continuation of activities related to these seven objectives.	Operate structure/network. Evaluate effectiveness in relationship to this objective and refine structure and activities as needed.	Operate structure/network. Evaluate effectiveness and refine as needed to ensure that it continues to have a positive impact.

Westerly, RI, CPP Team

Objectives (numbers do not reflect priority order)	Short Term— Spring 2000	Next Year— 2000–2001	Long Term— 2001–2003
5. Parenting classes and support groups on topics such as typical/atypical development and how to access needed services. These build on existing programs and are offered in various ways with schedules to meet varied families' needs, e.g., typically unserved and underserved, those who cannot attend programs on weekdays, at-home moms and dads, and/or offer hands-on activities such a field trips beneficial to both child and parent.	Develop action plan and initiate implementation related to identifying and coordinating options that are currently available in our community.	Implement action plan related to expanding parenting classes and support groups. Evaluate activities.	Refine action plan/ activities and continue to implement as long as activities are having a positive impact.
6. Resource materials associated with topics in the vision in various formats (e.g., print, video) for parents. Materials could be included in the gift bag, used as part of training and support groups, etc.		Develop action plan to address location and/or resource development to support objectives one and five. Evaluate materials.	Refine action plan/re- sources and continue to implement as long as resource materials are having a positive impact.
7. A Birth to Six Early Childhood Center that is a site for (a) direct service programs (e.g., Early Intervention, child care, Head Start, public school services), (b) parent training classes, (c) parent support groups, (d) family oriented programs, (e) resource materials (centralized for commu- nity), and (f) single point of contact for families.		Develop action plan and initiate plan implementa- tion (e.g., plans for center we would like to see, potential costs, potential funding sources, etc.)	Implement action plan, including a plan for evaluating effectiveness of this center.

Which way to go? *Does the team have enough information on which to base decisions about priority setting or to move from priority setting to Action Planning?*

Directions: Sometimes, teams need information in addition to the initial team assessment of the current community context (SWOTs) in order to make decisions about priorities to pursue or how to pursue them. Depending on the nature of the information needed, the needs assessment can occur:

- Prior to priority setting;
- After priority setting in order to get information needed for Action Planning; or
- As an initial strategy/action step in the team's action plan.

The team can gather this information from existing sources, e.g., federal, state, or local government; agencies participating on the team; or research. It can also design processes of its own.

SOUVENIR

South Kingstown, RI, CPP Team Needs Assessment Strategy

This team conducted a survey of blended early care and education services for young children and their families as an early step in one of their action plans. Two team members conducted this via phone interviews to learn how other communities were "blending" funds from different payors to provide comprehensive early care and education services to young children within the age range of birth through age five. The questions were developed, in part, based on a request for information from the Board of Education and the superintendent. Questions were crafted during a team session with the superintendent. Sites

selected in Kentucky, Colorado, and Illinois for interviews were identified by CPP staff. Information obtained from this survey helped the team (1) see concrete examples of other communities achieving blended services much like the South Kingstown vision, (2) learn strategies for blending services and funding sources (e.g., state child care funding, parent fees for child care, preschool special education funds, state education funds for at-risk children, Head Start funds, education funds under Title I, and Even Start), and (3) get practical advice from others "in the trenches." Later the team used questions such as these to guide their visits to programs with blended services in Rhode Island and Connecticut. A copy of this survey appears at the end of the South Kingstown Team Profile appearing in Chapter IX.

SOUVENIR

The Denver, CO, CPP Team transitioned from challenge identification to Action Planning by coupling challenge identification (issues/concerns) with brainstorming major strategies. They used this information as the foundation for Action Planning. As described more fully in their profile in Chapter IX, they referred to this activity as C.A.R.T.ography—Mapping Our Journey.

Denver, CO, CPP Team

Challenges	Strategies
Identification and Eligibility • Lack of concern for parental involvement. • Need to deal with time/process barriers for categorically eligible children.	• Build relationships during home visits. • Provide training from parent perspective. • After initial referral, clarify minimum information needed to proceed and communicate with all parties.
Service Coordination • Confusion! Too many players. • Clarify roles and responsibilities for each service coordinator.	• Players need to define roles and how they are overlapping. • Clarify process from first contact.
IFSP • Lack of fluidity in process and forms that do not reflect change. • Too many different forms.	• Come to consensus about process and create consistency about process regardless of entry point. • Collaboration between families and agencies to create a uniform form.
Transition • Kids falling through cracks: not enough information shared. • Confusion and inconsistency regarding rules.	• Identify cracks/gaps and those kids. • Create task force with timelines—write down what each agency does, educate community resource providers.

Action Planning

Which way to go? *What are the action plan components through which the team addresses the identified challenges? What are strategies the team can use for action plan development?*

Directions: In order for the vision to be realized, the team must develop a clear and specific plan for each of the challenges identified as priorities for immediate team action. Recommended components include:

- *Objectives* that are measurable statements of what the team wants to accomplish in order to overcome the challenge(s) and move toward its vision;

- *Strategies/action steps* to achieve each objective;

- Person(s) responsible for each strategy/action step;

- Resources needed for each strategy/action step (if applicable);

- Timeline for each strategy/action step; and

- Outcome that articulates how the team will evaluate whether they have accomplished their objective.

The action plan ultimately becomes the "road map" that the team can use for tracking activities and recording the outcomes and impact of the strategies.

Backseat Driving:

Tips for Action Planning

Action plans are a task analysis of things that must be done to carry out the plan strategy and achieve the objective. For example, a *challenge* might be that staff are not consistently implementing transition policy and effective practices. An *objective* might be to provide multifaceted, interagency, and job-embedded professional development to increase staff knowledge and skills related to transition policy and practice. *Strategies* and *action steps* are then the specific "to do list" of things to set up, implement, and evaluate the professional development leading to people exhibiting transition knowledge and skills through consistently implementing transition policy and effective practices (the challenge is overcome).

Plans should be specific enough to guide the team's work and keep it accountable, and yet, the team should also be flexible, adjusting the plan as needed based on new information that may result from plan implementation and evaluation.

Collaborative Planning Team Action Plan Form

Team: _____

Vision: _____

Challenge: _____

Period Covered by Plan: _____

Objective	Strategies/ Action Steps	Resources	People	Timeline	Outcome

This form may be reproduced without permission.

Instructions for Collaborative Planning Team Action Plan Form

Team: _____

Vision: *What you want to see at some point in the future (usually three to five years) as a result of challenges having been overcome. In effect, what you are working toward. This may be the total vision statement or that part of the vision relevant to the challenge being addressed in this action plan.*

Challenge: *A problem you are trying to solve that is standing in the way of achieving your vision, e.g., staff lacking the knowledge and skills that they need to perform critical functions.*

Period Covered: *Generally one year*

Objective	Strategies/ Action Steps	Resources	People	Timeline	Outcome
Tangible things your team wants to accomplish to overcome the challenge and move toward vision, e.g., parent training and support groups, transition policies and procedures, community resource directory, committee/ structure to address interagency issues on an ongoing basis, mechanism for communicating with physicians on child and system basis, etc.	For each objective, list the series of steps that your team will need to take in order to accomplish that objective.	Identify the resources (money, people, training, materials, etc.) that you will need in order to implement your action plan. Your strategy column should include steps to access the resources.	Identify the people who will be responsible for implementing each step in the strategy column.	Identify the timeframe during which each step in the strategy column will be completed.	Identify how you will evaluate whether you accomplished the objective. Leave blank space in this column for the team to use for documentation: • Did you do what you said you would do? • Did it produce the results you wanted? • What have you learned as a team as a result? • What are the next steps?

Activity

Action Planning Activity

1. Appoint a team facilitator, recorder, and timekeeper.

2. The **recorder** makes "Header Cards" and posts them on the storyboard that is two sheets of flip chart paper high and two sheets wide so that it looks like this:

   Action Plan Objective:

   Strategies/Action Steps   *Resources*   *People*   *Timeline*   *Outcome*

3. The **facilitator** asks team members to generate strategies on note cards to respond to the following focus question:

   What are strategies/action steps we should undertake to help us achieve our action plan objective—that will take us toward our vision? These strategies relate both to what the team will do to produce the desired product, policy, service, etc. and also what the team will do to ensure that individuals and agencies have the capacity for full plan implementation in a way that will truly address the identified challenge and take the team toward its vision.

4. If the group is four people or less, participants can respond as individuals. If the group is five people or more, have them work in "small groups" of two to five members (depending on the size of the group) to generate strategies. If the facilitator is a team member, he or she may also participate in this activity either as an individual or as part of a small group.

5. Participants/small groups write with markers on the cards. WRITE ONLY ONE STRATEGY OR ACTION STEP PER CARD. If you are using small groups, give them about 10–15 minutes to talk about and agree to the strategies/action steps that their group wants to share. It is helpful to set a timer (e.g., a kitchen timer) or have a **timekeeper** remind them how much time they have left at various points in the activity to help keep them focused.

6. When time is called, participants take their cards up to the board and post them on the storyboard. They do not need to worry about sticking them under the Strategy/Action Steps column. They can just place their cards anywhere on the storyboard.

7. The **facilitator** leads the team in reviewing the strategies/action steps that have been generated and removing any duplicates. In some cases, you may decide to merge two or more common strategies/action steps into a new statement. In this case, the team's **recorder** will write this new strategy/action step on a card and give it to the facilitator for posting.

8. Once the team has nonduplicative strategies/action steps, the **facilitator** leads the team in putting these in order/chronological sequence under the Strategies/Action Steps column. That is, what will we do first, then second, etc. As you post the cards, DO NOT overlap the note cards. Just place them close

Activity

Action Planning Activity *(continued)*

together, one under another. In doing this sequencing, the team will likely determine the need to rewrite a strategy/action step, add one, or delete one. The **recorder** will write revised/new strategies/action steps as needed and give to the facilitator for posting.

9. Once the Strategies/Action Steps column is complete, the **recorder** puts blank note cards under each of the header cards of columns remaining.

10. The **facilitator** reviews each strategy/action step and asks the team as a whole:

   • **Resources**—What, if any, resources do we need to carry out this strategy/action step (e.g., a survey, people whose input we need, fiscal resources, meeting space, etc.)? The facilitator or recorder records the response. If no resources are needed, leave the card blank. Do not remove the card.

   • **People**—Identify the people who will be responsible for implementing each strategy/action step in that column.

   • **Timeline**—Identify the time frame for completing the strategy/action step.

   • **Outcome**—Identify how plan implementation will be evaluated. It is also suggested that some blank space be left in this column so that the team can use it for documentation. As you proceed with plan implementation, review the action plan at each team meeting, making notes in this column regarding:

      • Did we do what we said we would do?

      • Did it produce the results we wanted?

      • What have we learned as a team as a result?

      • What are the next steps?

This activity may be reproduced without permission.

COLLABORATIVE PLANNING TEAM ACTION PLAN—

This action plan addresses one challenge of the Cranston, RI, CPP Team. It was developed via the process outlined above. It addresses not only what the core team will do (develop a universal release form), but also what the team will do to build the capacity of individuals and organizations regarding plan implementation (form use) and to track and evaluate plan implementation. Note that the plan also addresses the exit of the CPP facilitator and the team operating on its own. A full copy of their plan regarding all challenges and the resulting universal release form appear with the Cranston Team Profile in Chapter IX.

Collaborative Planning Team Action Plan Form

Team: Cranston, RI   **Period Covered:** March 2000–June 2001

Vision: As a collaborative team representing Early Intervention, child care, Early Head Start, Head Start, and public schools, we are committed to increasing collaboration among agencies providing early education and care so that these services are seamless, inclusive, and adequate in quantity and quality to meet the needs of ALL children ages birth through kindergarten age (age six) and their families.

Challenge: The adoption of *common forms* supporting these interagency transition policies and procedures (e.g., use of a universal release of information form) would facilitate communication and make agency requests for information from parents and providers less duplicative.

Objective	Strategies/ Action Steps	Resources	People	Timeline	Outcome
1B. Adopt *common forms* supporting these policies and procedures (e.g., use of a universal release of information form) to facilitate communication and make agency requests for information from parents and providers less duplicative. NOTE: Other forms (in addition to universal release of information form) will be developed as needed as part of the action plan for 1A (overall transition policies and procedures).	1B.1 Obtain: • Existing releases from each agency. • Forms from other states. We have VA form and direction from RI (Interagency TA Guide blue section). • Information on what is legally required from a state/federal perspective and through local agency policies and procedures.	• Agency releases. • Releases from other state. • RI Interagency TA Guide legal side-by-side for state/federal requirements. • Local agency policies. • State EI/DOH policy person.	• ALL Team members • COZ (Child Opportunity Zone)	Homework *prior to 9/14 meeting:* Locate and bring 12 copies to the meeting.	At 9/14 meeting, forms obtained for: At 9/14 meeting, legal requirements obtained for:

Collaborative Planning Team Action Plan Form (continued)

Objective	Strategies/ Action Steps	Resources	People	Timeline	Outcome
1.B. Continued— Adopt *common forms* supporting these policies and procedures (e.g., use of a universal release of information form) to facilitate communication and make agency requests for information from parents and providers less duplicative.	1B.2. Meeting agenda: • Review agency forms regarding commonalities and differences; identify features we like/don't like. • Define types of information we want/need to share and why (for which release will be used). • Identify form parameters (legal requirements impacting the form, essential items vs. non-essential items, how long form is good for, etc.). • Design or select/ adapt a rough draft of a common template that can be shared electronically.	Parent input via advisory board representatives attending our 9/14 meeting.	Team members, facilitated by Dennis, will invite a parent representative from their respective agency advisory groups: Cranston Special Education Advisory Committee, Project READY Advisory Committee, Head Start Policy Council, other advisory committees as appropriate.	9/14 Team Meeting, Noon–3:00, Project READY Office at Gladstone Elementary *(It may be necessary to spread these tasks over two meetings.)*	9/14 Team Meeting Outcomes:

Collaborative Planning Team Action Plan Form (continued)

Objective	Strategies/ Action Steps	Resources	People	Timeline	Outcome
1.B. Continued— Adopt *common forms* supporting these policies and procedures (e.g., use of a universal release of information form) to facilitate communication and make agency requests for information from parents and providers less duplicative.	1.B.3. Circulate draft form for comment.	Get input from Cranston Cabinet and other individuals/entities as appropriate.	To be determined.	Within one month of form completion.	Feedback received on form:
	1.B.4. • Revise form as needed based on input received. • Make plans to resubmit form as needed to Cranston Cabinet and to get state officials' okay. • Identify types of people who will most typically use form. Design strategies to provide them with information/training.			Team meeting, date to be determined, Noon–3:00, Cranston Head Start. (This is last meeting facilitated by Peggy Hayden, CPP staff.)	Meeting outcomes:

Collaborative Planning Team Action Plan Form (continued)

Objective	Strategies/ Action Steps	Resources	People	Timeline	Outcome
1.B. Continued— **Adopt *common forms*** supporting these policies and procedures (e.g., use of a universal release of information form) to facilitate communication and make agency requests for information from parents and providers less duplicative.	1B.4. (continued) • Develop feedback mechanism regarding form so that form and procedures for its use can be revised as needed.				
	1B.5. Implement form use, training, etc. per plans developed at previous meeting.		Upon adoption of form.	Individual agencies via CPP team leadership.	Record of events regarding form training and dissemination activities:
	1B.6. Evaluate whether or not the team accomplished its objective, revising form and procedures for use as needed.		To be determined.	CPP Team Meeting	Evaluation of objective:

Which way to go? *Should the team confine Action Planning to the core team or involve other stakeholders?*

Directions: Some teams will start with multiple challenges to be addressed through multiple action plans. If developing multiple action plans at the same time, teams can choose to conduct planning via Action Planning teams composed of:

- Core team members only (as most of the CPP teams chose to do), or

- Core team members and other stakeholders as the Denver, CO, CPP Team and the South Kingstown, RI, CPP Team chose to do.

As noted in Chapter IV, even if Action Planning is restricted to core team members, the team can get the input of key stakeholders through various means, e.g., surveys, interviews, conversations at staff and parent meetings, review of previous studies, etc. This is very important in order to ensure that action plans are relevant to the people who will be impacted by the plan (implementers and consumers).

SOUVENIR The Central Falls, RI, CPP Team used a survey to get the input of staff and families on the direction they should take in their action plan to establish a Centralized Data Bank of Community Resources, a place that people could visit or contact by phone or computer to find out what kinds of community resources are available to families of young children in Central Falls. They developed a "Survey Regarding Establishing a Central Falls Centralized Data Bank of Community Resources." They collected information both from individual respondents and from passing the survey out at staff and parent meetings for completion during the meeting. This facilitated the team getting a very good response. The survey was in both English and Spanish. The English version appears at the end of the Central Falls Team Profile appearing in Chapter IX.

If the team chooses to use Action Planning teams composed of core team members and other stakeholders, the teams should be chaired or co-chaired by members of the core team to help facilitate communication between these two types of teams. Action Planning teams are task groups composed of five to 12 key stakeholders, such as practitioners and consumers, who have the knowledge to develop effective strategies to address their assigned challenge (Daniels, 1986). Using such stakeholders in addition to core team members helps to link planning to the "level of use," that is, using input from the people who will actually implement or be impacted by plans (particularly line staff and families) (Fullan, 1993, 1991).

Backseat Driving:

Tips for Involving Noncore Team Members on Action Planning Teams

Involve people who have a stake in the outcomes of the action plan topic, such as people:

- Whose support you need, such as agency heads or representatives of agencies who are not regular team members; or

- Who will be involved in implementing the changes necessitated by the plan, such as administrative and direct service staff; or

- Who will be impacted by the plan, such as families.

If the team is developing multiple plans all at the same time, it can use the following "Round Robin Activity for Editing Multiple Action Plans." This activity can be used with both types of action plan teams, that is, those composed of core team members only and those composed of core team members and other stakeholders. Using this activity will result in all team members having input into and being aware of all action plans, thereby promoting relevance and buy-in. It will also facilitate continuity among various individual action plans, because plans can be edited after the Round Robin Activity to ensure that plans complement each other.

Activity

Round Robin Activity for Editing Multiple Action Plans

Purposes:

1. To help the team achieve consensus on action team plans IF the team develops multiple action plans addressing multiple challenges.

2. To help the team review all action plans to get a sense of the "big picture" so that final plans resulting from the action teams are relevant to multiple people/agencies and are congruent across all of the team's action plans.

Preparations:

1. This activity takes place at a point when initial drafts of multiple action plans have been developed and are posted on flip chart paper on which cards are posted with the various components of the plan as follows: (see previous Action Planning Activity)

   Action Plan Objective

Strategies/Action Steps	**Resources**	**People**	**Timeline**	**Outcome**

2. Each of the action plan teams that actually developed each action plan draft is assigned a different colored marker with which to makes edits, e.g., Team One will be making edits with a red marker, Team Two with a blue, and so on. It is also helpful to have 4" x 6" sticky notes and extra note cards that can be used, where necessary, for recording new ideas or idea modifications.

Instructions:

These instructions presuppose that the team has three action plans with team members divided among the three action plans, preferably with members being the actual people who developed the action plan draft, that is, it is "their" plan. The actual number of action plans will vary depending on the team's priorities and might range from two action plans to several. If this is the case, adapt the following activity according to the number of plans you actually have.

1. Each team assigns one person to stay behind as **"home team" facilitator**, while the rest of the team moves to another team's work.

2. Each team rotates so they have a chance to review and comment on the work of all other teams. Set time allocations for each rotation. 10–15 minutes is usually adequate. If you had 3 teams, it would operate as follows:

	Team 1	**Team 2**	**Team 3**
Round 1 is at	Station 1	Station 2	Station 3 (Home)
Round 2 is at	Station 2	Station 3	Station 1
Round 3 is at	Station 3	Station 1	Station 2
Final Round is at	Station 1	Station 2	Station 3 (Home)

Activity

Round Robin Activity for Editing Multiple Action Plans *(continued)*

3. When a new team arrives, the **"home team" facilitator** clarifies but does not defend "home" team ideas. The visiting team edits ideas by asking themselves, "Can we live with and publicly support within our own agencies the ideas that we see posted here?" If not, the team should edit the ideas by:

   (a) Adding new ideas;

   (b) Deleting or marking through (but not eradicating) ideas; or

   (c) Otherwise modifying the home team's ideas.

   Each team can edit any work appearing at the station—even putting back in ideas another team deleted. They should review the People column if their names are mentioned on another team's plan in order to confirm that this is something they are willing to do. If their name is NOT assigned to a strategy in which they have an interest, they should be encouraged to sign up.

4. The **"home team" facilitator** listens to the visiting team's comments, asking questions as needed to seek to understand their rationale for their edits. When the set time has expired, teams rotate to the next station, continuing to do so until they have visited each team's work and returned "home."

5. When teams return to their home stations, the **"home team" facilitator** leads them in a debrief through which the team attempts to come up with a final set of recommendations that reflect ALL the teams' ideas. These are then presented to the large team for a final review which is usually able to accept the recommendations fully or with only minor edits.

This activity may be reproduced without permission.

Which way to go? *Do the agencies and individuals identified as having some role in plan implementation have the capacity to carry out those roles?*

Directions: Action plans should be a "to do" list for core team members to achieve the objective. They should also build the capacity of the individuals and agencies related to knowledge, skills, and structures that they will need in order to implement team plans and successfully address the challenge on which the plan is based. For example, if the challenge includes (1) difficulties in sharing information among agencies, and (2) duplicative agency requests for information from parents and providers, it is not enough to develop a universal release of information form. Team plans must also

ensure that agencies and individuals have the capacity to use this form to ensure:

1. Staff and families know how to use the form (e.g., staff and parent training, inclusion in staff and family handbooks, instruction sheet regarding form completion);

2. Individual agency adoption (e.g., the form is incorporated within respective agencies' policies, procedures, and forms);

3. The form is actually being used (e.g., periodic record review); and

4. Plan implementation is eliminating the priority challenges (problems with information sharing and duplication) so that refinements can be made if needed

(e.g., mechanisms to evaluate form use such as staff and family surveys or interviews, or staff meeting discussions).

Thus, action plans should address not only the development of services, plans, policies, and products by the team. Plans should also include strategies and action steps to ensure that agencies and individuals (service providers and consumers) will have the capacity needed to implement the team's plan. The Cranston, RI, CPP Team action plan cited earlier in this chapter is an example of an action plan that addresses this issue. More information on supporting plan implementation appears in the next chapter.

Are We There Yet?

Advice on helping teams evaluate their progress and evolve to the next stage.

The team should ask itself the following questions:

1. Were clear, objective, mutually agreed-to criteria used in determining priority challenges?

2. Do the challenges chosen represent a significant barrier to the vision?

3. Did the team "think big and start small," setting priorities that are doable given team members' available time and resources and likely to result in a quick and public victory?

4. Which Action Planning approach did the team choose: Action Planning by the core team or Action Planning through Action Planning teams? Did the team choose to develop action plans for one priority challenge at a time or multiple challenges? How has this worked?

5. Regardless of action plan approach, have strategies been used to ensure that action plans are relevant to the stakeholders who will be impacted by the plan (implementers and consumers)?

6. Are action plans written in such a way that people know what they need to do step-by-step in order to accomplish the plan's objective? Do the plans include the necessary components?

7. Do action plans address not only the core team's "to do" list to develop a plan, policy, service, or product but also strategies and action steps to build the capacity of the individuals and agencies related to the knowledge, skills, and structures that they will need in order to implement the plans and successfully address the challenge on which the plan is based?

Chapter VII

Being on the Road

Implementing Plans, Allocating Resources, and Evaluating Accomplishments and Teamwork

O nce action plans are written, the team should celebrate. However, this is not the end, but the beginning of the plan implementation stage. This is where the facilitator's ongoing efforts in building the team's capacity to work together effectively pays high dividends by ensuring that team members have the knowledge, skills, and structures necessary to work together as a team and to sustain the team through the tasks of plan implementation, resource allocation, monitoring, and evaluation. These tasks are not distinctly separate steps but rather inter-related functions to support the desired change that the team hopes to accomplish to take them toward their vision.

SOUVENIR

"Having these plans is very important to give concrete and specific direction to who needs to do what when, etc. However, completing the plan is only the beginning. Achieving the action plan outcomes necessitates having a variety of strategies in place and adapting those strategies as needed. As the team begins implementing plans, it will learn new things, get new information or resources, get input from others, etc. This, in turn, will bring about the need to adjust plans and, even, the vision accordingly. Strategies need also to attend not only to 'getting the task done' but also to developing positive relationships within and outside of the team. The team should be sensitive to accommodating the workstyles and personalities of team members and the people in the community whose support the team needs."

South Kingstown, RI, CPP Team

To paraphrase Senge (1990), plans don't perform, people do. Teams need strategies to ensure that plans are actually implemented. They need to ensure that people know what to do, know how and when to do it, and have the necessary resources. They also need mechanisms to evaluate whether or not plan implementation is having the desired impact on identified challenges and how well the team is functioning.

This chapter discusses:

1. Implementing action plans;

2. Allocating resources; and

3. Monitoring and evaluating team accomplishments and teamwork.

SOUVENIR

"Some communities meet and never do anything. This one does! The team had lots of enthusiasm, because we were tackling issues that had been problems for us for a long time and we wanted to resolve them. We were not afraid of hard work."

Westerly, RI, CPP Team

Implementing Action Plans

Which way to go? *How can the team support agencies and people in making the changes required in the plans? What are strategies for building motivation and intervening positively with resistance?*

Directions: Plans by their very nature require people to change some of their current practices. Team plans may call for following new procedures, using new forms, implementing new intervention or instructional strategies, providing new services, or working with other agencies and families in new ways.

People do not automatically get "on board," embracing the changes called for by the plan. Research shows that as change is initiated, there is a "creative tension" between how people have always done things and the vision they want to create (Senge, 1990). Their vision pulls them forward if the vision is meaningful to them. It motivates them to try new ways of doing things. However, until they have some success at implementing the change, they may express resistance to the proposed change. Moreover, change implementation will require new competencies—knowledge and skills. Their initial lack of competence may erode implementers' confidence and initial enthusiasm for collaboration, and comments may be heard such as, "Things were so much easier the old way."

So what can teams do? Like breaking any old habit and developing a new one, implementing change takes time. As referenced in Chapter II, people go through various stages of concern, decision, and behavior related to the change or innovations (Hall, Wallace, & Dossett, 1973). The core team should ensure that team members within each agency and the core team itself have ongoing job-embedded professional development, supports, and incentives for plan implementation to address these various stages and ensure that people have the knowledge, skills, and attitudes that they need to implement the change (Rous, Hemmeter, & Schuster, 1999). Stages of implementer needs related to change and corresponding team supports are depicted in Figure 1.

Figure 1
Stages of Implementer Needs Related to Change and Corresponding Team Supports

Implementer Needs	Team Supports
Wanting to be made aware of the proposed change	Awareness sessions and materials
Wanting more in-depth information	In-depth training, ongoing job-embedded professional development and materials
Deciding how to incorporate the change into what they do	• Planning, practice, and reflection time • Resources needed for implementing change • Opportunity to network with other implementers • Supervision • Feedback on staff performance and consumer benefit
Building it in to one's routine	• Planning and reflection time • Opportunity to network with other implementers • Supervision • Feedback
Refining the change based on practice and feedback data	• Planning and reflection time • Supervision • Feedback
Networking with others for ideas and support	• Opportunity to network with other implementers • Information sharing mechanisms: newsletter, listserv, website, e-mail, etc. • Staff meeting discussions • Study groups/committees to work on special aspects of plan implementation • Recognition via agency or team events or publications (media coverage, newsletters, memos, certificates) • Release time for program visitation
Finally, adapting the change or deciding to take on new changes	• Professional development • Recognition • Planning time

Backseat Driving:

Tips for Building Capacity of Individuals and Agencies

- Support both individual and organizational development, including ongoing job-embedded professional development for staff and families.

- Professional development on an interagency basis is time- and cost-efficient, reaches a broader audience, and has the added benefit of fostering positive working relationships among people across agencies.

- Conduct cross-program visitations for staff and/or families so they can become familiar with the various community services. This helps expand their perspective beyond that of one agency to a broad collaborative community picture. In short, they meet their "community partners." If time is not readily available, such visits can be carried out by having speakers from other agencies, reviewing brochures of other agencies, or, if available, taking a "video tour."

- Provide feedback and follow-up support balanced with pressure to achieve results.

SOUVENIR

Collaborative Training for Staff and/or Families

Acadia Parish, Crowley, LA: The Pre-K team (members include CPP team members) put on a collaborative inservice day on curriculum for Even Start, Head Start, and public and private preschools in the area. Head Start and Even Start staff took colleges classes together.

Denver, CO: Provided technical assistance via a forums series explaining transition processes for families, joint staff meetings, and trainings on transdisciplinary methods.

Greater Metropolitan Clark County, Las Vegas, NV: The team brought in national speakers to learn more about providing natural environments and learning opportunities.

South Kingstown, RI: Initiated compilation of a calendar to coordinate existing parenting programs and to serve as a tool for identifying service gaps.

Westerly, RI: Established a family awareness series via radio broadcasts and workshops regarding typical/atypical child development. Workshops were held at various early childhood agencies with child care being provided. They provided an ongoing story hour for families of young children under the age of three at the Westerly Parent-Teacher Resource Center.

Which way to go? *How can the team effectively manage and coordinate plan implementation? What happens to the action plans once they are written? What is their relevance to team meetings after they are written?*

Directions: Continue monthly meetings to coordinate plan implementation. Rather than setting the finalized action plan aside, make it a living document by using it to guide team activities and build agendas for each meeting. That is, according to plan timelines for each month's meeting, on what strategies and action steps should the team anticipate hearing a report and by whom (person responsible)?

SOUVENIR

"The plan is the guide for the team's work—not a piece of paper to be set aside when done. As the team's guide, it helps keep the team on task and accountable. Of course, it can be adapted as needed in light of changing contexts and information learned during implementation."

Cranston, RI, CPP Team

Backseat Driving:

Tips for Maintaining Team Documentation

Create a team folder with various files or a notebook for:
- Meeting agendas and minutes.
- Team mailing list and member information (profiles, brochures, fact sheets).
- Ground rules, interagency agreement/policies, procedures and forms.
- Team plans.
- Team products.
- Resources for access by team.
- In team ground rules, identify who will maintain the "master" folder/notebook and how this will be used to orient new members.

Which way to go? *How can the team track and document plan implementation and team decisions?*

Directions: Document team learnings and decisions in writing. This helps reinforce a common understanding of and commitment to issues on which there has been agreement. It also facilitates implementation, activity tracking, and evaluation. In addition to written action plans, other options for documenting team decisions include written interagency collaborative agreement(s), incorporating areas of agreement within individual agency contexts and documents, and commonly adopted forms.

One option is a written interagency collaboration agreement, often referred to also as a memorandum of agreement (MOA) or memorandum of understanding (MOU). It is required by some federal or state laws. To be more than just "another piece of paper to be in compliance," this agreement should not be an end in itself but rather be a document that reflects collaborative planning and problem solving. Moreover, it should be a fluid document that evolves from year to year as changes occur among the collaborative agencies and related to the various areas on which they are collaborating. This chapter provides a Generic Format for an Interagency Collaboration Agreement that communities can adapt as needed.

Generic Format for an Interagency Collaboration Agreement

Explanation: *The following is a generic format for an interagency agreement.* **Bolded items** *reflect topics typically included in such agreements.* **Nonbolded items** *provide instructions for the user regarding adapting this format to meet unique community needs.*

Interagency Collaboration Agreement

Participating Agencies (List agencies signing the agreement):

I. **Purpose of Collaboration**—Briefly describe the reason for the collaboration addressed in this agreement, such as to achieve a shared vision, provide high quality services to children and families, maximize resources, meet community needs, etc.

II. **Period Covered by the Agreement**—Identify when the agreement will take effect and when reconsideration of the agreement will take place (unless reconsideration is requested sooner by any of the participating agencies).

III. **Brief Description of the Collaboration**—Summarize the basic nature of the collaboration. Potential areas of collaboration include, but are not necessarily limited to, the following 12 collaboration areas:
1. Family involvement;
2. Child Outreach/Child Find, screening, referrals, and evaluations;
3. Service eligibility;
4. Individual program planning (e.g., Individual Family Service Plans and/or Individual Education Programs);
5. Primary and related services delivery (if the collaboration is for the purpose

77

of blending direct services among two or more agencies, include a description of the proposed model, number of days, hours per day, service area, agencies involved, services to be provided, numbers of children to be served, etc.);

6. Service settings that, to the maximum extent possible, work with children in natural settings typical for the age of the child and which educate children with disabilities along with children without disabilities;

7. Resource sharing including, but not limited to, facilities, materials, equipment, collaborative services, screening, etc.;

8. Transition;

9. Confidentiality;

10. Records transfer;

11. Joint staff training; and

12. Sharing child count data.

IV. **Applicable Legal Requirements**—Indicate if this agreement is pursuant to any state or federal legal requirements. If so identify policy, regulation, statute, etc. and who will be responsible for ensuring compliance.

V. **Contact Person(s) in Each Participating Agency**—For each participating agency, indicate by position title, persons responsible for decision-making and problem solving for each agency related to the collaboration agreement. Provide contact information for these people, current as of the date of the agreement signing.

VI. **Participating Agencies' Responsibilities**—For each participating agency, describe activities, timelines, and persons to be held accountable. A variety of formats may be used for providing this information:

- Topical listing in narrative/paragraph form in which a collaboration area is identified (e.g., Child Find), followed by the respective responsibilities of each of the participating agencies.

- Agency listing in narrative/paragraph form in which each of the participating agencies are listed. Under each agency, all responsibilities relevant to the agreement are listed.

- Chart format in which the areas of collaboration are listed down one column with applicable participating agencies' responsibilities being listed across corresponding columns.

VII. **Mechanism for Coordinating Agreement Implementation**—Describe how participating agencies will coordinate agreement implementation, including provisions for how:

1. Decisions will be made and by whom, and

2. Representatives from the participating agencies will meet to plan activities and resolve issues as they arise. Include a schedule for meetings and a list of who should attend.

VIII. **Evaluation and Program Improvement**—Delineate the schedule and process for evaluating the outcomes and impact of the collaboration, including how this information will be used for program improvement. This should be done preferably by a team comprised of representatives from participating agencies. It should include formal and informal feedback on progress and needs for change from administrators, staff, and families directly involved in the collaboration as well as data on child impact, as appropriate. Include an agreed-upon process for annual assessment of the partnership itself.

IX. **Resource Sharing**—Include a description of resources that may be shared, such as direct services, facilities, materials, equipment, personnel, food services, transportation, training resources for staff and/or families, etc. As described previously under the section on "Participating Agencies' Responsibilities," a variety of formats may be used for providing this information.

X. **Amendments to the Collaboration Agreement**—Indicate what process will be necessary and who will need to sign off on amendments.

XI. **Termination of Agreement by Either Party**—Indicate the process by which the agreement can be terminated. Include timelines, notifications, and authorization required.

XII. **Signatures**—For each participating agency, provide that agency head's or his or her designee's signature, name (typed), title, agency, and date.

This form may be reproduced without permission.

SOUVENIR

Interagency Agreements

Denver, CO: Interagency Memorandum of Understanding for Part C Service Coordination among Denver Public Schools Child Find, Denver Health Children and Families Program, Denver Early Childhood Connections (Part C), and Denver Options (Community Center Board) to clearly define a process to assure that all eligible families receive the same information, assurances, and options regardless of which agency provides service coordination and to assure that each family is provided with one service coordinator. This agreement, entitled Interagency Community Partnership for Part C Services Coordination in Denver County, appears at the end of the Denver Team Profile in Chapter IX.

St. Vrain, Longmont, CO: Interagency agreements articulated by way of flowcharts for both Child Identification (format in Chapter IX) and for Transition.

The team should also consider incorporating areas of agreement within individual agency contexts and documents. For example, participating agencies' policies and procedures should reflect commonly agreed-to collaborative procedures. Individual agency calendars can reflect collaborative events and/or common timelines for transition or other areas of collaboration. Staff job descriptions can include responsibilities related to collaboration. These strategies help to increase individual agency buy-in, particularly beyond the administrative level. In fact, sometimes it is more feasible to institute policy, procedures, and practice changes working through individual agencies than securing agency head signatures on an interagency agreement.

In many instances, commonly adopted forms are the easiest and most time-efficient method for implementing areas of common agreement. Using the same form facilitates communication among agencies and provides continuity for families as they move from one service agency to another. Also, forms are usually easier to change than formal agreements.

Common Forms

Cranston, RI: Universal release of information form to facilitate information sharing and to minimize paperwork for families and agencies where children and families are either dually served and/or transitioning from one agency to another.

Denver, CO: Common IFSP form and shared consent form.

St. Vrain, Longmont, CO: Single intake form for families (in process), universal referral/consent for release of information (in process), and updated developmental checklist with contact information.

Which way to go? *How can the team keep key stakeholders informed about plan implementation? What are strategies for communicating plan implementation information and decisions within the team, among those impacted by plan implementation and with the community at large?*

Directions: Develop mechanisms to ensure ongoing communication within the team, among those impacted by plan implementation, and with the community. Minutes, memos, newsletters, and related communication devices can be used to transmit information on collaborative activities and areas of agreement to a variety of audiences including participating agencies' leadership, staff, families, state agencies, and the community at large. Materials that describe the team are beneficial for sharing with families and other service providers. Such materials may include a brochure describing the various agencies, the team vision, and/or purpose. The team can also use other public awareness activities to not only achieve the goals of those particular activities but also as a way to build community awareness about the team and public support for early childhood services. Such activities might include Child Find, Week of the Young Child, Open House, Kids Day, Family Night, Information Fair, etc. It is helpful to build a relationship with a journalist who is willing to write an article on team activities and to whom the team can send periodic updates. Personal contact is best. Ask him or her for tips on getting publicity for the team. This chapter includes a sample press release that teams can adapt to publicize their efforts.

SAMPLE PRESS RELEASE

Headline: Such as

Our Community Celebrates Week of the Young Child

Local Team Promotes Quality Services for Young Children and Their Families

Communitywide Screening of Young Children Planned

Local Early Childhood Team Attends State Training

A team of people in our community are working together to promote comprehensive, high quality, inclusive services for young children and their families. This team is known as

_____.

Team members include (insert names, titles, and agencies) _____

_____.

Insert paragraph(s) explaining the activity you want to publicize.

Include this paragraph if applicable: Over the years, this team has worked together on many successful activities. Previous accomplishments include _____.
Current team priorities include_____.

If you would like more information on this team or services offered through participating agencies, contact _____.

This form may be reproduced without permission.

Many teams promote community awareness about team efforts and early childhood resources through the development of a service directory as a resource for participating agencies, families, and/or the community at large. The Agency Profile provided in Chapter IV is a good starting point for this. Directory development as an initial activity has these benefits:

- Helps team members learn about each other (they really don't know as much about each other as one would think);

- Provides them with information on current community services, which also serves as a form of community needs assessment;

- Is low risk and low cost;

- Can be used immediately as a resource with staff and families;

- Results in a concrete product (evidence of collaboration) that does not take an undue amount of time to produce;

- Provides positive public visibility for the team and individual agencies; and

- Builds the team's capacity to work together toward a common goal.

SOUVENIR

Service Directories

Acadia Parish, Crowley, LA: *Acadia Parish Early Childhood Resource Guide* made available in hard copy to staff and families.

Central Falls, RI: Directory in hard copy, on computer at the community Family Support Center, and via the local school district website.

Cranston, RI: Directory developed in conjunction with their Family Resource Center known as a COZ (Child Opportunity Zone) disseminated in hard copy to families and staff. They are computerizing this directory.

Denver, CO: Directory took the form of two resource matrices, one for services in general and one related to child identification. The team has identified the need for a common information base and a computer person to link databases among agencies.

South Kingstown, RI: Worked with regional educational collaborative Child Find staff to develop a directory in hard copy and on computer on the school district's website.

St. Vrain, Longmont, CO: Resource matrix developed for staff use in planning. They plan to adapt this for family use.

SOUVENIR

Joint Child Find/Child Outreach and Public Awareness (in addition to service directories)

Acadia Parish, Crowley, LA: Participated in the public schools' "Literacy Walk," a public awareness campaign on the importance of reading. Each family participating received a free book.

Central Falls, RI: Developed a "single stop" resource and referral phone line at the community Family Support Center staffed by bilingual personnel along with a computerized service directory of early care and education resources and a refrigerator magnet in English and Spanish to use as part of a program to educate parents and others about the availability of this resource and the resource and referral phone line.

Greater Metropolitan Clark County, Las Vegas, NV: Developed plans for a marketing campaign with the theme, "Las Vegas families love their children!" Distributed Part C Child Find materials to help families of young children with disabilities and at-risk conditions to locate services.

South Kingstown, RI: Collaborated on Child Find resulting in extensive early screenings: incoming public school kindergarteners, 3–5 year olds, and all Head Start students. Planning to develop an "Early Childhood Care and Education Newsletter" promoting community support for early childhood initiatives of the CPP team and individual CPP agencies to be disseminated strategically to key agencies, families, community leaders, civic organizations, the business community, etc.

St. Vrain, Longmont, CO: Developed a Child Identification Activities Flowchart listing different child identification activities and agencies that provide general, vision, or hearing screening, or developmental evaluations. Established a single point of entry.

Westerly, RI: Purchased a developmental wheel with milestones birth-5 which includes tips for parents related to child development and immunizations for dissemination to families via multiples options, e.g., CPP team member agencies, public library, physicians' offices, gift bags, community fair, etc. Developed a "prescription pad" referral form for physicians for referrals to either the school district's Child Outreach (Child Find) Office or to Early Intervention. Met with 15 local physicians during hospital rounds to heighten their awareness of early childhood community resources and the CPP team's desire to collaborate with physicians via the "prescription pad." CPP team members collaborated with a physician's group on a five-session parenting series. The team collaborated on an early childhood display at a school district community fair, providing gifts bags and information for families on early childhood services.

Which way to go? *How can teams deal with "implementation dips" and keep people motivated?*

Directions: Invariably, initial team enthusiasm will wane. Fullan (1991) refers to this as the "implementation dip" in which "things get worse before they get better and clearer as people grapple with the meaning and skills of change" (p. 91). Anticipate this dip and plan strategies in advance to address it when it inevitably comes. It helps teams to know that while such a dip feels bad, it is developmentally normal and, with appropriate intervention, should be temporary. Times when dips are likely are (1) when one major task has been accomplished and the team is needing a "second wind" to get restarted; (2) at the beginning of the school year after some team members have been on summer vacation and the team is needing to recharge and refocus; and (3) when there is a turnover in key members, the loss of whom makes the team feel fragmented (because they temporarily are).

At points such as these, team members should reflect on the vision, accomplishments to date, and how accomplishing objectives has/will benefit them and the children and families they serve. An implementation dip can also occur if the task seems overwhelming, because it is too large or because staff are unsure how to go about implementation. If the task is too large, break it down into smaller steps effecting change by successive approximation and providing implementers with a way to track and see progress. Use professional development strategies noted previously to provide staff with implementation support.

Finally, integrate the change into existing programs to ensure people can see how the change fits into their picture rather than seeing it as some "irrelevant tacked on special project" that will go away if ignored. Help them see "What's in it for me?" not by telling, but by having discussions through which they discover the benefits. If they are able to see the benefit to themselves and the children and families they serve, they are more likely to stay motivated.

Backseat Driving:

Tips for Helping People Stay Motivated and See What's In It For Me (WIIFM)

Have a guided team discussion around questions such as these (adapt as needed). Work through each question, one at a time, having team members generate responses on cards individually or working in small groups, posting on a storyboard, and then reviewing as a team (using the storyboard approach as described in Chapter III).

- What are the activities our team has implemented thus far?
- What activities have been the most effective? What factors made them so?
- What have been the benefits thus far for yourself and the children and families you serve?
- What are new activities we will soon be implementing (or challenges we are facing)?
- If implemented effectively, what will be the benefits for you, children, and families?
- What are learnings from previous activities that we can use in addressing new activities (challenges)? What are other good ideas to try? What are needed resources or supports?
- What will be at least two things that you will try next?

SOUVENIR

"Our team experienced what many teams do, that is, the need to reignite enthusiasm to maintain the team after its initial organization. This was particularly true after summer vacation during which a number of the team members were not working or on vacation, making team meetings difficult to have when everyone could attend. We addressed this by having a meeting at the beginning of the school year at which the team reviewed our vision and accomplishments to date. That inspired us."

South Kingstown, RI, CPP Team

Allocating Resources

Which way to go? *What is meant by the term "resources?" Is this only money or does it mean other types of resources as well?*

Directions: Action plan development and implementation should include resource allocation to ensure that people have the means they need for plan implementation. Resources can take many forms. They can be copies of policies, procedures, or forms. Resources can include instructional materials for use with children or as part of staff or parent training. For example, the team can establish a loan system that can be a place—a lending library—or a system such as an annotated listing of materials and equipment agencies are willing to share as a result of contacting that agency. Resources can be space in which to carry out collaborative activities or services. Time is an important resource and agencies will need to support staff in finding the time to do these "new" activities and incorporate them into their existing schedules. Resources may also refer to better utilization of existing services through blended or coordinated services. Finally, depending on the nature of the plan, the team may also need to figure out how it can pool existing funds or perhaps even locate new funding for collaborative activities.

Which way to go? *What will collaborative plans cost? Will collaboration require a grant or new funding? What if community agencies do not have "extra" resources to commit to collaboration?*

Directions: Most teams are able to accomplish much without any "new" money. Many activities can be carried out as part of the regular job roles of various team members. To this extent, personnel, facility, and operational support (e.g., team mailings, office supplies, meeting space) are provided on an in-kind basis by the team members. Assuming team priorities are consistent with the mandates or priorities of the respective agencies on the team, it will likely be permissible to use existing funds for collaborative purposes. That is, one agency may be able to pay for printing a service directory as part of its Child Find budget or another agency may be willing to expand the scope of its resource and referral line to address team priorities, because this is consistent with its mission. Sometimes, all agencies contribute to covering costs associated with their particular agency. For example, each agency agrees to pay for printing the collaborative release of information form to be used in their own agency and cover the tasks of staff and parent training in that regard, because this is a mandated function anyway.

Which way to go? *How can a community offer new services without new money? How can collaborative services be financed?*

Directions: Collaborative services can be provided through "blending" services. Rather than needing new funding, services are operated in new ways using existing funding streams from individual agencies. Team staff from individual agencies may work together to carry out their existing functions previously done as a separate agency in the past. This allows them to improve and/or expand services such as screening, assessment/evaluations, transition planning, home visits, or parent training. A number of CPP teams had as a long-term goal the establishment of a community early childhood center offering comprehensive and inclusive services. In such a center, children would not be labeled according to funding streams, but rather just be labeled as "children." Staff would figure out how to use multiple funding streams to meet their needs. During the project, South Kingstown came closest to this goal and it remains a goal toward which other teams are actively striving.

SOUVENIR

Blending and Coordinating Existing Services

Acadia Parish, Crowley, LA: Head Start and Even Start have been working together closely since being involved in CPP. In addition, most of the original CPP team members are now part of the community's Pre-K team that is working to develop a consistent curriculum for all young children in the parish to achieve program continuity from one agency/program to another.

Cranston, RI: Head Start and public schools are working more closely together.

Denver, CO: Early interventionists are working collaboratively with school district staff to assess children, to plan for families on the waiting lists, to ease transitions, and to provide jointly staffed home visits. They have adopted an interagency agreement, common forms, and common procedures related to service coordination to eliminate duplication and enhance practices including ensuring that each family is provided with one service coordinator.

Greater Metropolitan Clark County, Las Vegas, NV: Head Start and public schools are working more closely together.

South Kingstown, RI: (all of the blending below came about because of CPP):

1. Co-location of a variety of services (inclusive pre-school services, Head Start preschool class and parent training program, early intervention, Parents as Teachers, Child Outreach/Child Find) in a public school facility along with a second Head Start class at another elementary school that collaborates with the kindergarten in that school.

2. Collaborative educational playgroups include (a) Head Start and Early Intervention; (b) Early Intervention coordinated with South Kingstown Parks and Recreation; and (c) Parents As Teachers bi-monthly playgroups at the YMCA, which Early Intervention parents attend.

3. CASSP blends a program on children's mental health with the YMCA.

4. The YMCA offers child care for families with kindergarteners, making full day services available.

Westerly, RI: See information later in this chapter on blending services provided under grants. In addition, team members have worked together on a community basis pursuing National Association for the Education of Young Children (NAEYC) accreditation for public school preschools and kindergartens, Head Start, and child care programs to improve program quality and to promote continuity and philosophical compatibility among agencies/programs (several are now accredited).

Which way to go? *Are there funds for which teams can apply on a collaborative basis? Who serves as the fiscal agent? Does the team need to be incorporated?*

Directions: Collaboration expands resources available for all in that an eligible grant applicant may be only one of the community agencies, but the resources can be used to have a broad impact communitywide. Many government agencies, foundations, civic and charitable groups in the community, and businesses look favorably on funding collaborative efforts. In fact, CPP teams discovered that once they had articulated their action plans, they had the basis for a grant proposal already done in large part. Then, when a funding opportunity presented itself, they "translated" these plans into the grant application format. In all instances, one agency served as the fiscal agent and the CPP team served as a grant advisory or management committee.

Acquiring New Grants to Support Collaboration

Central Falls, RI: Linked with another community collaborative endeavor through which a Head Start grant was accessed to print their service directory and purchase refrigerator magnets to publicize their directory and dedicated resource and referral phone line for accessing services.

Denver, CO: Wrote a grant to build greater community capacity for timely eligibility and evaluation through play-based assessments.

South Kingstown, RI: The CPP team is in the process of submitting a budget request to the Board of Education for continued and expanded use of the public school facility for their blended services and for an Early Childhood Coordinator position for the 2002–03 budget (this position does not now exist).

Westerly, RI: They secured their first Parents as Teachers (PAT) grant operated in collaboration with South Shore Mental Health and located at the Parent Partnership Program of the Westerly School Department, fiscal agent for the project. They also secured their first Even Start grant funded through the Westerly School Department to support team goals using a "cluster approach" to services through which Even Start services are provided in existing community partner agencies: (1) Head Start, (2) the public library English as a Second Language (ESL) program, (3) Early Intervention Program, using its building for a program for parents of children ages birth–three with the potential for having an inclusive program there, and (4) YMCA.

SOUVENIR

As part of plan implementation, the Central Falls, RI, CPP Team investigated options and issues associated with establishing its Central Falls Family Partnerships Directory. They used their action plan Outcomes column to monitor plan implementation and to record the outcomes of their investigations (strategies/action steps implementation), learnings, and decisions along the way. As time passed, they decided they needed to summarize their direction into a document to share with (1) other key stakeholders in order to encourage directory use along with circulation for directory information and refrigerator magnets to their families and staff, and (2) another community group that had funding that was ultimately tapped for purchasing the magnets, directory printing, etc. Drawing on their action plan, they developed a document entitled, "Central Falls Family Partnerships Directory Implementation Plan by the Central Falls Collaborative Planning Team," which appears in Chapter IX.

Monitoring and Evaluating Team Accomplishments and Teamwork

Plan monitoring and evaluation includes tracking plan implementation to see what is being done, what is being learned, and what plan refinements need to be made. The team should also track external variables (e.g., new mandates, funding sources or cutbacks, staffing issues) so that these can be integrated into the current context and aligned with and used for plan refinement—rather than losing focus and leaving the plan half implemented while they move to the new "issue du jour."

In addition to evaluating the outcomes and impact of plan implementation, the team should evaluate itself. It should assess how well members work together, how well their ground rules are working, whether their membership appears appropriate to the priorities they have chosen, and how well they are conducting their meetings.

Finally, plan monitoring and evaluation should also involve key stakeholders. That is, for change to be truly effective, it must be both top-down and bottom-up, balancing both external and internal motivation of those impacted by the plan (Fullan 1993, 1991; Senge, 1990). Hopefully, stakeholder

---

Backseat Driving:

Tips for Locating New Funding

• Use the Internet to search funding sources.

• Make contact with the development office at a nearby university. Ask them for advice on grant writing and on how to locate information on government and foundation grants for which the team might apply.

• Identify civic organizations and businesses in the community that have philanthropic priorities similar to those of the team, e.g., early childhood, children with disabilities. Investigate if these are linked to a national organization or foundation so that support can be solicited at both the local and national level. It is ideal when these investigations can be carried out by someone closely associated with the civic organization or business, e.g., a staff person or family member who is a member of the civic organization, a family member who is an employee. Civic organizations and businesses may also be the source of support other than or in addition to funding. They may supply volunteers for special projects. They may offer expertise, e.g., a local advertising club helped one team develop a brochure. Some businesses have a storehouse of furniture and office equipment that they may be able to donate. Some businesses may be willing to donate supplies, e.g., items to go into gift bags, door prizes for special events, etc.

• Research state and federal grants that are geared toward collaborative endeavors. These investigations can be done through the hierarchy of the agencies participating on the team, through the Internet, etc.

• Seek funding from local government or charities. It is helpful to precede such an approach with an effective public relations campaign to build community awareness and support.

• Do your homework. Find out about the funding source so that the funding request will respond to their agenda as well as the team's. Find out what expectations are for submitting requests. If possible, meet with someone to seek advice on proposal submission and to build a personal relationship. Have a clear proposal in mind that is succinct and that avoids jargon. Emphasize the concrete benefits that will result for children and families.

• In approaching local government or local or in-state civic organizations, businesses, or foundations, focus not only on the funding request but also on building positive relationships, being respectful, patient, and willing to compromise. Don't be offended with an initial no. Be gracious, thanking them for their interest. Keep them informed to plant seeds for the next time. If funded, thank them formally, e.g., a letter, plaque, some token developed by the children, public presentation with publicity in the local media. Follow-up later to inform them about how children and families benefited from their generosity to give them reinforcement they deserve and to strengthen relationships so that they will be more open to considering a future funding request.

involvement has addressed this issue during action plan formulation. Likewise, information should be collected from plan implementers and consumers and analyzed on an ongoing basis to determine plan status and impact. This will assist the team in keeping their direction relevant to stakeholders impacted by the plan. It will help them adapt the plan to the ever evolving context and ensure that adequate supports are in place until the planned changes are adequately institutionalized—at which time, these changes will become a foundation on which to build plans for new changes.

Which way to go? *How can the team ensure that plans are being implemented as planned? What if some element of the plan does not seem to be working? What if new issues emerge that the team had not anticipated—both those that relate to the plan and those that might get the team off track?*

Directions: Use the team's monthly meetings to track, report, and evaluate the implementation of collaborative activities. Record this status in the Outcomes column on the plan. Keep in mind that the plan is a road map and not a "compliance document." That is, the plan represents the team's best ideas for leading to its objectives, but the team is not expected to have a crystal ball. It is a given that plan implementation will result in unforeseen problems and successes. It will also produce new insights among team members. The team should anticipate that this will be the case and try to accept problems or new insights as inevitable and not as evidence of plan inadequacy. In short, don't get discouraged. Rather, revise the strategies/action steps as needed to address the problem or capitalize on the success and new insights in a timely manner. As the team implements its plan, opportunities or threats will likely emerge in the current community contexts, e.g., new mandates, new grants or declining resources, personnel turnover, etc. The team should try to balance staying focused on its commitment to the plan and attending to this changing context. Rather than "dropping the plan," whenever possible, the team should revise its plan to take these changes into account so that the plan will stay relevant.

> **"The monthly meetings provided consistent times for different members to connect and receive feedback about the quality of services provided. Instead of waiting until the end of the project to make the system change, these small system change pieces continued to happen throughout the year."**
>
> *Denver, CO, CPP Team*

> **"We feel that it is very important to formally evaluate progress at key points, determining both if we accomplished what we set out to do and if those accomplishments have moved us toward our vision. It is also important for the team to routinely dedicate a small amount of time at its meetings to have a conversation in which we reflect on what we are doing. These reflections help team members develop mutual understandings of what we are experiencing and keep the team on common ground. Finally, remember to frequently dwell on accomplishments! Celebrate!"**
>
> *South Kingstown, RI, CPP Team*

Finally, as the plan accomplishes its objectives or has other successes, recognize the contributions of team members and celebrate. Recognition and celebration help build the team's sense of effectiveness and momentum to keep going.

Backseat Driving:

Tips for Recognizing and Celebrating Team Accomplishments

Depending on the nature of the accomplishment:
- Celebrate it at a team meeting or some special occasion outside of work;
- Recognize team accomplishments and members in the local media and/or in respective agency newsletters or similar publications; or
- Provide team members with a certificate or some other token of appreciation.

Which way to go? *Is the plan producing the desired results? Are the identified challenges being addressed in a way that takes the team toward its vision? Is the team operating effectively? Is membership still appropriate? Are all team members doing their part?*

Directions: In addition to ongoing plan tracking and evaluation, the team should formally evaluate its overall operation at least annually related to the team's accomplishments and challenges, operational structure, and team member relationships and involvement. The following questions are recommended for periodic and annual review.

Questions for evaluating team priorities:

1. Did the team do what it said it would do? Is it achieving its objectives? How well? Are team activities beneficial enough to warrant the time and other resources allocated to them?

2. Is working on these priorities benefiting both the collaborative team/community and the participating agencies?

3. Do previously set priorities continue to be relevant to all members of the team? What priorities remain or are emerging?

4. What changes, opportunities, and threats in internal (agency) and external (community, state, federal) environments are likely to impact priorities of this team?

SOUVENIR The South Kingstown, RI, CPP Team facilitated the school district's decision to engage a consultant to gather longitudinal data on previous public school preschool and kindergarten graduates and to design a child outcomes evaluation model to be embedded in early childhood expansions as they move forward. The team also compiled national efficacy data for sharing with the local board of education.

The following Sample Evaluation Plan can be used for evaluating individual or multiple action plans in relation to achieving team objectives.

Sample Evaluation Plan

Plan Objectives	Audience (Who needs evaluation results?)	Measures (What data will be collected and how?)	Informants (Who will provide evaluation data?)	Timelines	Results (Based on data, to what extent is the objective achieved?)

This form may be reproduced without permission.

Questions for evaluating the team's operational structure:

1. Are meetings a good use of people's time? If so, what makes them so? If not, what can be done to improve them?

2. Is the team adhering to its ground rules that establish criteria for judging how effectively members work together as a team? Are these still relevant?

3. Are meetings being held at a regular and convenient time and place?

4. Are team roles clearly defined?

5. If the team is using a committee structure to address various priorities, is this working? Does it need to continue? If the team is not using a committee structure, would such a structure help the team be more efficient or would it make the team more cumbersome?

6. How is the team involving other stakeholders? How supportive are they? What does the team need to do to continue or strengthen this involvement to ensure that team plans remain relevant to the people whose support the team needs to ensure effective plan implementation?

Questions for evaluating membership involvement and team dynamics:

1. Are all members actively involved? Why or why not?

2. What can be done to get active involvement of all members?

3. Do activities or memberships need to change so that active involvement of all members will be more likely?

4. As new individuals or agency members are added to the team, what is done to help them adapt to the team and to help the team adapt to them (e.g., orientation or refocusing priorities to address new members' interests)?

SOUVENIR

NOTE: *This was the first meeting of the St. Vrain Early Childhood Council CPP Team's second year of operation. The CPP facilitator had exited in Spring 2001 and the team had decided to hire a consultant to facilitate their meetings so that all team members could be full participants. These minutes are edited slightly for inclusion in this manual. They provide a good example of (1) a well-run purpose-driven meeting, (2) a meeting that is grounded in full participation of all members, (3) effective minutes, (4) an activity for evaluating the meeting, and (5) an example of a team evaluating their first year of operation and planning for the new school year.*

St. Vrain Early Childhood Council

Educational Services Center, Board Room, St. Vrain School District

September 18, 2001 Minutes

Plans for Next Meeting: October 16, 2001, 9:00–Noon; Educational Services Center, Board Room; Homework: (1) Each person reviews last year's minutes and accomplishments; (2) How does it reflect the suggestions from this meeting? What are we missing?

Members Present: (Listing provided)

Team Purpose: Collaboration and support

Today's Purpose: (1) Regroup; (2) Confirm goals and successes; (3) Draft an action plan; (4) Create meeting structure and schedule for the coming year

Introduce Yourself: Each member shared (1) role and relationship to the team; (2) expectations for today; and (3) feelings about being here

Challenges We Face This Year

1. Growth

2. Lack of resources

3. Bond issue that could lead to new funds for expanded early childhood services

4. Struggle to work and make decisions for families without family representation

5. Staffing, low wages, need for systematic change

6. Careful about "group think" instead of each individual child's situation

7. Head Start money at risk at federal level

8. Federal money may be at risk

9. We should not rely on jargon—what do our words look like?

10. Actions toward moving toward best practice

11. Growing diversity

SOUVENIR

What Are the Behaviors, Skills, and Actions That Have Helped Us Be Successful?

(*Areas we will need to focus on in 2001–2002).

1. Trust each other*
2. Follow through—do what we say*
3. Blend leadership styles
4. Consistent attendance
5. Overall commitment*
6. Everyone participates
7. Active listening
8. Humor
9. Good leadership—logistics, coordination
10. Treat each other with respect
11. Good food
12. CPP staff facilitation
13. See results
14. Very positive and upbeat
15. Targeted outcomes*
16. Patience and move purposefully*

Review of Goals and Successes

Goal I: Develop a collaborative system to ensure the availability and accessibility for early identification of children with special needs or who are at risk for future developmental concerns.

Goal II: Develop a collaborative system for child and family supports: (1) Agreement; (2) Continued support; (3) Relationship and understanding; (4) Education—knowledge information.

What Are the Accomplishments, "Prouds," and Successes From the First Year?

1. Resource/phone matrix
2. Identified "social service" kids as "at-risk"
3. Single point of entry; Child Find marketing strategies; Child Find flow chart
4. Single intake form for families (in process)
5. Universal referral/consent for release of information (in process)
6. All children: Weld County and Boulder County for Child Identification
7. Interagency agreement regarding Part C Transitions
8. Improved understanding of what everyone does (in process); know each other better, both what is there but what isn't (gaps)

9. "Staying on Track" brochure being improved by CO Department of Education (on which we had input) (in process)
10. Warm Welcome updated developmental checklist with contact; widened participation base
11. Organizational flowchart (in process)
12. Emphasis on bilingual needs—for monolingual families
13. Doubled CPP slots
14. Referrals from Mental Health and Department of Social Services

The Vision—How Will We Know We Have Been Successful 1–3 Years in the Future?

Identification

- We will know what the process flow is.
- A family can go anywhere, physicians, and agencies and obtain immediate information.
- Families will immediately know resources.
- Phone number information at the tips of all fingers.
- Families do not have to wait more than two weeks.
- Family receives information and feels in control.
- Service coordinator follows family.
- Child Find includes 0–2.9 years.
- A lot of communications, a lot of buzz. Universal consent happening; lack of duplicate efforts, respecting family's confidentiality.
- Agencies use data collected by others and evaluations to best meet child and family needs.
- Intervention.
- Funding would flow smoothly—birth on.
- Blended funding.
- Flexibility in criteria and problem solving.
- Attention to all kids (needs special education, at risk, all); other risk factors considered.
- A vision is in place.
- Sufficient program slots for preschool and Head Start.
- Sufficient three-year-old classrooms.
- Early childhood community center for one-stop shopping.

Strategies and Actions to Get Us There

- Brochure "Staying on Track" generously distributed via plan addressing turnover, different levels of community people.

SOUVENIR

• All documents are in Spanish/English.

• Create our own identity, logo, and letterhead.

• Team/cadre of speakers/trainers, building awareness with providers, front line people.

• Finish flow chart—develop a presentation.

• Advocacy with decision/policy makers— problems regarding resources, growth, staff turnover.

• Know and support each other and articulate services; BCMC-BCAYC connections; Pilot group—early child care and educational task force; Center of St. Vrain Valley.

• Standardized intake, referral, and consent forms; investigate how each agency is writing/approaching; share with each other, different groups, and counties.

• Promote the Week of the Young Child in April (speakers, learning, etc.).

• Educate childcare providers regarding "risk factors"—trauma effects on brain, other issues.

Suggestions Related to Structure for Our Meetings:

• Clarify strong vision and goals

• Prioritize

• Time—focused projects; action team—focused (review in relationship)

• Mini-teach by educating ourselves; presentation on matrix; mini-teach on acronyms

• Address bond issues related to funding St.Vrain's vision, Tiny Tim's vision, etc.

Meeting Schedule for the Coming Year: The St. Vrain Early Childhood Council meetings are held from 9:00 a.m. until noon on the third Tuesday of the month, with the exception of November and February for which alternate dates have been chosen. A schedule was prepared for these monthly meetings including dates, locations, and persons responsible for snacks at each meeting.

Evaluating Our Time Together:

I appreciate

• The renewal of old friends and the beginning of new friendships

• Facilitation

• The welcoming group

I liked

• The way we work

• The addition of a new member

• The expansion and focus of all kids

I am concerned about

• One county had only representative

I wish/hope we

• Brought my minutes

• Celebrate

Which way to go? *When the team completes implementation of its plan, what then?*

Directions: Once the team has completed implementation of its plan, evaluation results will help the team chart its next course. Perhaps, the context is such that the team will consider itself "finished" and, therefore, the team will disband. Hopefully, however, the team will be able to take learnings from this collaboration and continue to work together to address new challenges toward its initial or a revised vision. If the team decides to continue its journey toward new "destinations," it should use the same strategies it used during its initial formation to set priorities and develop action plans. It should also reevaluate its membership to ensure that the team is composed of the right people needed to address the team's new priorities.

Backseat Driving:

Tips on Team Evaluation

• The team, if formed properly, was initially pulled together in order to have the "right people" together to address a particular focus or priority. As priorities of the team change, it is important to discuss if the people need to change too. Perhaps some members will no longer find the team relevant as it addresses these new priorities. Perhaps new members will need to be added. Revamping membership should in no way be considered as a negative but rather as a practical strategy to ensuring effective teamwork and not wasting people's valuable time.

• As the team "reforms" around new priorities and/or membership, use this manual in charting new direction.

Are We There Yet?

Advice on helping teams evaluate their progress and evolve to the next stage.

This chapter has presented extensive information on how teams can evaluate their progress and evolve to the next stage. This information underscores that a collaborative team is not a static entity. It evolves over time as there are changes in individual and agency membership, changes in funding and regulatory structures, changes in the community, or new needs emerging among children and families. Team interactions will also evolve as team members develop a history of working together. Hopefully, celebrating successes in addressing initial challenges will create team momentum. Relationships and team insights from early collaborations will serve as a foundation for addressing more complex and comprehensive challenges resulting in meaningful systems change ultimately leading to the team's vision of a better future for young children and families.

Chapter VIII

Checking the Rearview Mirror

Lessons Learned

Ｔhis chapter provides CPP staff reflections on lessons learned related to:

1. Helping teams transition from one facilitator to another;
2. CPP top ten rules of the road for facilitating collaborative teams; and
3. Concluding remarks.

Helping Teams Transition From One Facilitator to Another

Whether internal or external to the team, the original team facilitator will eventually move on. For example, an internal facilitator's "term" may expire and this person may assume some other role on the team. There may be turnover. Or, if an outside facilitator is used, circumstances may cause this person to no longer be available.

Plans should be put in place for this facilitator transition. From the start, team members should not become dependent on one individual. The facilitator (whether external or internal) should design activities that enable all team members to practice facilitation skills. Ideally, as time progresses, various team members can begin to assume more and more of these responsibilities.

By the second to last meeting with the exiting facilitator, the team should decide which team member(s) will assume this role. Some teams decide to share this role rotating that responsibility from meeting to meeting. However, most teams choose a facilitator or cofacilitators to serve an annual term, referring to this person as facilitator(s), team chairperson(s), or some similar title.

In anticipation of this change, at the final meeting the facilitator should help the team plan for this transition through:

1. Clarification of the priorities on which the team will be working along with an action plan for doing so (likely a plan already developed/in progress);

2. Confirmation of the team's meeting schedule and locations for the next meeting and those in the near future (e.g., for the remainder of the school year);

3. Determination of the purposes of the next meeting and a tentative agenda for that meeting (e.g., use the Collaborative Team Organizational Meeting Agenda in Chapter III or other agenda model as a guide); and

4. Evaluation and celebration of their accomplishments.

SOUVENIR

"It will be important as we move forward to keep people involved by choosing tasks that are meaningful to them and to the team as a whole."

Cranston, RI, CPP Team

Backseat Driving:

Tips for the Facilitator in Exiting From the Team

- Choose a team member(s) to assume facilitator responsibilities.
- Design activities to have team members practice facilitation skills prior to facilitator's departure.
- At the final meeting, help them identify their insights on teamwork and celebrate achievements.
- At the final meeting, plan for the first meeting after the facilitator's departure.
- If an external facilitator is leaving, have them remain available to the team by phone or email, touching base with them every four to eight weeks for several months to check status and to offer encouragement and, if requested, advice. If feasible, contact them approximately six months after facilitator departure (or some key juncture for them)—preferably through a meeting with them—to reflect on their progress and learnings and how these can be used to enhance future collaborations.

CPP Top Ten Rules of the Road for Facilitating Collaborative Change

1. **You can't mandate what matters.**
   - The more complex the change, the less it can be forced.
   - Mandates are important. But, for desired change to become reality, people must act. For action to occur, people need not only external motivation (e.g., mandate) but also internal motivation (they see the need).

- People need a plan for implementing the mandate or change along with the necessary knowledge, skills, resources, and a feedback loop to ascertain if the change is beneficial.

SOUVENIR

"While not visible, there are 'boundaries' that separate state agency representatives from local program directors, and as such, they do not operate as equals or colleagues in a functional sense. Thus, state agency representatives may encourage the development of a local vision, but they can not impose their vision upon the locals. Ultimately, state level representatives must find ways to cultivate leadership at the local level so that the vision resulting in systemic change is homegrown."

*Greater Metropolitan Clark County
Las Vegas, NV, CPP Team*

2. **Collaborations must be needs driven, context embedded, and fueled by accomplishments.**
   - Collaboration is not an end in itself. Use it as a means for team members to resolve a common problem/address issues of mutual need.
   - New policies, procedures, forms, services, or activities proposed by the team should be embedded in the current context in order to be sustainable over time.
   - For collaborations to be successful, they must be based on needs perceived as important and relevant to the collaborators.
   - Involve stakeholders beyond the core team whose support is needed for implementation in planning and evaluating the collaboration so that plans will be based on their needs and relevant to their contexts.
   - There are various methods of effectively involving stakeholders. Choose those that are meaningful both to those stakeholders and to the team.
   - To support team momentum and motivation, celebrate accomplishments and provide various forms of meaningful recognition for the team, participating agencies, and individual contributors.

SOUVENIR

"Each agency in this rural, low income area was well aware of the needs and challenges of stretching resources. The CPP team meetings provided a chance for individuals to think outside the specific demands of their daily work and look at the early childhood system comprehensively. With few additional resources, they were able to compile a very detailed and user-friendly resource guide to increase accessibility to the resources available in the community."

Acadia Parish, Crowley, LA, CPP Team

3. **Local collaborations are facilitated by both top-down and bottom-up support.**

While people at the local level are the ones who must ultimately plan, implement, and evaluate the collaborations, state agencies can support local collaborations via:

- Demonstrating that collaboration is a priority through resource allocation, policies, and modeling collaboration at the state level;

- Training, technical assistance, and other resources;

- Recognition such as showcasing sites;

- Opportunities for networking and mentoring among sites;

- Clarification of legal or other issues that appear to be collaboration barriers; and

- Providing fiscal resources for collaborative initiatives.

SOUVENIR

The state level Rhode Island Early Childhood Interagency Task Force used its annual statewide conference on early childhood collaboration to showcase the efforts of CPP sites and other collaborative endeavors and to facilitate networking among local teams. Collaborations in additional communities were stimulated as a result. The Task Force also provided an Interagency Technical Assistance Guide including a side-by-side of legal requirements, suggested collaboration strategies, information on key resources in the state, and local team profiles and samples.

SOUVENIR

CPP teams impacted state systems as follows.

Acadia Parish, Crowley, LA: CPP Team members are now part of a statewide task force to develop performance indicators for all Pre-K students in Louisiana.

Denver, CO: They identified service coordination and its lack of "coordination" as the team's biggest challenge. They communicated that to the state, which responded by dedicating resources to statewide training/TA for core competencies on service coordination, rewriting state guidelines for using family resources and insurance, and working closely with the Denver team to create an understanding of funding streams and a hierarchy for using different resources.

St. Vrain, Longmont, CO: Provided input as a team on revisions to the Colorado Department of Education's "Staying on Track" brochure.

4. **Commitment to collaboration evolves over time as a result of people working together on mutually beneficial activities.**

- As much commitment as possible is desirable at the beginning, but in reality, initial buy-in is commitment "in concept."

- Genuine commitment comes after the team has worked together long enough to see team results that they perceive are worth their time.

- Commitment is a by-product of successful collaborations.

SOUVENIR

"After working together over time, we no longer see kids as belonging to any one agency. These are Westerly's kids."

Westerly, RI, CPP Team

5. **Build a team vision and goals based on assessment of the current community context.**

- Make the vision as concrete and doable as possible so that it will seem real to team members and not just "words on paper."

97

- It will be easier for people to think about how they would like to see things in the future (vision) if they assess first what is happening in their current context.

- Although the team should articulate a vision early on, a "true" and meaningful vision will take time to emerge, evolving after team members have had a chance to have success at working together and begin to have team "a-ha's" about the possibilities that collaboration can bring. When the vision becomes truly meaningful, it will ignite dedication to stay the course even when obstacles appear.

SOUVENIR

We have made so much progress but also have a long way to go and much to do in this community. We just lost in the election that would have raised funds for an early childhood center and many more schools for the district. We'll try again next year!"

St. Vrain, Longmont, CO, CPP Team

6. **Think big and start small.**

- Thinking big helps the team cultivate a "systems" perspective and see how the challenges they are addressing fit into the big picture of the community.

- The big picture is often too abstract for many people and can seem overwhelming—"we'll never be able to do that!"

- Starting small gives the team something concrete on which to work.

- Help the team choose initial activities that will give them a quick and public victory.

SOUVENIR

"Systems change doesn't happen in one electrical moment—seemingly small changes impact people and systems!"

Denver, CO, CPP Team

SOUVENIR

"We wanted our services to be 'a good fit' for families rather than forcing families to fit our services. We were able to break down barriers to accessing services in our community. Because of our work, families will no longer have to experience several intake processes and tell their stories several times."

Central Falls, RI, CPP Team

7. **Having an outside facilitator is not essential— but very helpful, particularly during the team's early stages. A "neutral" facilitator:**

- Is perceived by all team members to be nonpartial;

- Allows everyone to be a team member, focusing on accomplishing team work rather than having to be concerned about running the meeting;

- Can focus on helping the team build its capacity rather than promoting his or her agenda; and

- Should remain with the team until it is self-sustaining as evidenced by being organized as a team, having accomplished at least one concrete task, and having a plan for further collaborations. This can usually be accomplished in five to six meetings (one meeting every four to six weeks).

8. **Sustaining the collaboration requires at least one champion on the team who:**

- Is willing to provide leadership to bring the team together;

- Is committed to collaboration and making it work;

- Is perceived by the team to be fair, a good leader with the team's interest in mind (not only his or her own);

- Has good facilitation and organizational skills related to the mechanics of meetings, keeping the group on target; and

- Can carry on as facilitator if an external facilitator is used in the team's early stages and then leaves.

9. **Focus training, technical assistance, and team facilitation on capacity building.**

    - Help team members build positive working relationships.

    - Support learning how to operate as a productive team using effective meeting and organizational dynamics.

    - Build team member knowledge and skills related to the task(s) they choose to tackle, because plans don't perform, people do.

10. **Team facilitation is a developmental process with the facilitator's role evolving commensurate with the team's capacity.**

    - As the team is forming, the facilitator is a foundation builder.

    - When the team is storming and expressing differing perspectives, the facilitator is a referee/nominalizer.

    - When the team has solidified and is tending to focus more on socializing than working, the facilitator is a task manager.

    - When the team becomes high performing, the facilitator is an observer and process adviser.

    - When the team reaches a key turning point due to task accomplishments, changes in the community context, or membership turnover, the facilitator supports the team in reflecting on what it has done and how it

has worked together so that the team can transform itself in order to stay relevant to team member needs and the community context.

Concluding Remarks

This manual has been developed to provide rationale and resources for supporting the development and operation of effective local early childhood collaborative teams. It is hoped that local administrators, local Interagency Coordinating Councils (ICCs), and other local collaborative teams as well as state administrative and TA staff will find this a helpful "road map" in their journey toward meaningful change in local early childhood systems through the facilitation of collaborative services for young children and their families.

SOUVENIR

"There is no 'single answer' or 'simple recipe' to follow that will guarantee effective collaboration. Rather, collaboration is a process that the team has to experience by doing. The CPP model provides a frame for this process, but the team has to actually work through it, learning from the inevitable ups and downs of such a process. And when they do, 'many minds make great work!'"

South Kingstown, RI, CPP Team

Chapter IX

Looking Through Our Scrapbook

Profiles and Products From CPP Teams

This chapter provides profiles on each of the CPP teams along with some of their key products. These profiles provide information that is current as of the date listed at the top of each profile. In addition, toward the end of each profile, an update is provided that is current as of Winter 2001–02. The profile format is:

1. Team Description
2. Partners
3. History and Development
4. Results
5. Resources
6. Sustaining and Replicating (Carrying on after the CPP facilitator leaves)
7. Lessons Learned in Relation to the CPP Model
8. Where Are They Now (Winter 2001–02)?

Crowley, LA, Acadia Parish CPP Team Profile 1999–2000

1. Team Description—The Acadia Parish CPP Team was an interagency work group for collaboration and planning of comprehensive early childhood systems. Their goal was to increase educational opportunities for all children, birth through kindergarten.

During CPP participation, the team focused on developing a networking system and increasing public awareness of all available services for children, birth through kindergarten.

2. Partners—Team members originally consisted of about ten members representing the following agencies and organizations:

- Head Start parents
- Head Start teachers
- Even Start Home Visitors Program
- Acadia Parish School Board

- Child Search (Child Find)
- Title I
- Cooperative Extension Services
- Health

As the meetings progressed, the team decided to add important stakeholders—elementary school principals. Five principals attended meetings during the last half of the project year and added a critical component to the process. They were viewed as the end users of the early childhood system and their expertise was much valued.

3. **History and Development**—Acadia Parish is a rural area of Louisiana. Most team members knew each other, but hadn't met or worked together formally as an interagency group. They welcomed the opportunity to work together by responding to a state department of education RFP in April 1999 to participate in the CPP project. One person connected with the team wrote, "In order to promote the development and intellectual growth of the whole child and provide opportunities to empower parents to improve their parenting skills, there exists a need to formulate a well defined interagency collaborative decision making body within the school system."

Eight stakeholders attended the first meeting. A state department of education representative attended and encouraged the group to pursue more collaboration, especially with Head Start. The group developed a needs assessment that emphasized that parents are important and that they need support. The team decided to meet every two months. Twelve stakeholders attended the second meeting. They agreed to meet as a task force for one year and to make decisions by consensus. After working through an Environmental Scan the team felt strongly that principals needed to be invited, because they "receive" what early childhood systems "produce."

Five principals joined the stakeholder team. The team worked together to develop a vision with a written action plan as follows:

Vision: A networking system for all available services for children, birth through kindergarten.

Challenge: Coordination is informal, fragmented, and hard to understand.

Objectives: To outline components of and define responsibilities of the network. To raise public awareness for the networking system.

Strategies: Name and classify resources, analyze and look at models and examples of resource guides, directories, and websites from other places.

Resources: Intergovernmental agencies. Private sector. Related collaborative efforts. CPP Stakeholder team.

CPP provided the impetus for getting together and looking at early childhood services and resources as a comprehensive system. During the course of the year, over 22 different agencies and organizations participated in the interagency process. The team realized that the community of Acadia Parish needed an easier way to find and get access to resources for young children and families.

4. **Results**—The Team sent out surveys to all early childhood service providers in the parish. They used resources from several agencies to compile all the information received and produce the Acadia Parish Early Childhood Resource Guide. The guide details information on 20 different resources for day care centers, early childhood education, early intervention programs, and family programs including:

- Program contact information
- Sites of programs
- Target population
- Ages of children served
- Eligibility requirements
- Procedures for enrollment
- Preregistration dates
- Brief description of program
- Length of services
- Transportation provided

5. **Resources**—The time and energy of each team member contributed to the development of the resource guide. The Cooperative Extension Service added the guide to their resources provided to families in the area. The team also asked the state Department of Education to

print and help disseminate the guide to the following groups:

- Each person that returned a survey form
- Office of Family Services
- Office of Community Support
- Service coordinators
- Health units
- Youth sources
- Churches
- City hall
- Libraries
- Adult Education Building
- Homeless centers
- ASSIST office
- Mental health centers
- Housing Authority
- Doctor's offices
- Lower elementary principals

6. **Sustaining and Replicating (Carrying on after the CPP facilitator leaves)**—The team perceived value in their collaborative efforts and decided to extend their work beyond the original year-long commitment. They decided to work together to put on a fall Resource Fair for service providers, teachers, bus drivers, and families with young children. Continuing Education hours could be offered. A convenor was selected and future meetings were scheduled.

7. **Lessons Learned in Relation to the CPP Model**—

- *Think big and start small!*—The first versions of the Acadia Parish vision were all-encompassing and broad based. They were noble but overwhelming. The team prioritized and decided to focus on a project they could do together that would have the biggest impact on young children and families. Their final outcome—the Resource Guide—was an effective use of interagency resources that made access to community resources more available to young children and families.

- *The value of working together as a team*—Each agency in this rural, low income area was well aware of the needs and challenges of stretching resources. The CPP team meetings provided a chance for individuals to think outside the specific demands of their daily work and look at the early childhood system comprehensively. With few additional resources, they were able to compile a very detailed and user-friendly resource guide to increase accessibility to the resources available in the community.

- *The importance of determining key stakeholders*—The original team consisted of early childhood service providers and parents. They quickly realized that they needed to add people who made decisions that impacted services and families. Elementary school principals were perceived to be not only the end users of the early childhood system, but a very powerful influence for the community. Their participation provided much needed momentum to the team's work.

8. **Where Are They Now (Winter 2001–02)?** Although they have not met recently as a CPP team, collaboration continues formally and informally in many ways. In effect, the CPP team has not ended. It has just evolved in a new direction. That is, most of the original team members are now on the community's Pre-K Team that is developing a consistent curriculum for all young children in the parish. The Pre-K Team put on a collaborative inservice day in August 2001 to promote this curriculum for children attending Even Start, Head Start, and public and private preschools. That way the children can all start out on the same page when it comes time for assessment. It is noteworthy that issues of a comprehensive developmentally appropriate curriculum and staff development were part of the CPP team's vision. Former CPP team members are also part of a statewide task force to develop performance indicators for all Pre-K students in Louisiana. Head Start and Even Start have been working together closely since CPP. They are also taking college classes together. Head Start, Pre-K, Even Start, and public schools recently put on a collaborative Literacy Walk that was a public awareness campaign on the importance of

reading. Each family participating received a free book. Public awareness and family empowerment were also CPP goals. Finally, the team noted that it has been easier to go to the health department for assistance since CPP.

Central Falls, RI, CPP Team Profile
September 1999–November 2000

1. **Team Description**—The Central Falls, RI, CPP Team was a group of parents and professionals representing community agencies and the school district. This team came together to promote quality, inclusive, culturally competent and seamless early education and care services. Ultimately, this team wanted to ensure that early care and education services were adequate in number and type to fully address the needs of all young children and their families in Central Falls.

During CPP participation, the team focused on developing strategies to ensure that (1) all agency staff and families have equal access to a common set of information on community resources related to children and their families and (2) families have access to this information either via a key community agency (e.g., the agency with which they are already involved) or via a call to the resource and referral line.

2. **Partners**—
- Captain Hunt School, Central Falls Public Schools
- Central Falls YMCA
- Child Opportunity Zone (COZ), Central Falls Public Schools
- Early Head Start through Children's Friend and Service
- Early Intervention Services at Meeting Street Center
- Families with young children
- Head Start (Pawtucket/Central Falls Center)
- Head Start State Collaboration Project
- Progreso Latino
- Parents as Partners at Meeting Street Center
- Visiting Nurses Association of Care New England

3. **History and Development**—Although they had a history of collaborating from agency to agency, they had not collaborated as a communitywide team prior to becoming involved in the CPP. The CPP provided a mechanism to expand these existing community-school collaborations into a formal comprehensive, collaborative communitywide effort. As the team progressed, it merged with another collaborative effort in Central Falls known as the Head Start Early Care and Leadership Institute, since both CPP and this project involved similar participants and provided short-term resources that were used by the team as the basis for long-term benefit and collaboration. The CPP facilitator worked with this team from September 1999–June 2000.

4. **Results**—This team identified a number of barriers preventing families from accessing needed services. First, both agency staff and families frequently lacked common and current information about the various resources in their community. Families also experienced difficulties in knowing whom to contact for information, locating services or other resources. Or, if they contacted a particular agency that agency might explain that they could not help the family if the family were looking for a service not provided by that particular agency. Families sometimes had to experience the intake processes of several agencies in order to access the services they needed. The team wanted their services to be to "a good fit for families rather than forcing families to fit our services."

To respond to these service barriers, the team has developed a "single stop" resource and referral phone line along with a computerized service directory/databank of early care and education resources in the Central Falls/Pawtucket area. This will be in operation starting in the 2000–01 school year.

The team surveyed families and staff in multiple agencies to ascertain their needs related to this issue and used their input in carrying out their plans. They collected information both from individual respondents and from passing the survey out at staff and parent meetings for completion during the meeting.

They received a very good response. The survey was in both English and Spanish. The English version of this survey appears at the end of this profile. They used the statewide RI Traveler's Aid Directory as a base for their computerized service directory/databank and localized it.

They located the resource and referral phone line and computerized service directory/databank at the Family Support Center of Children's Friend and Service. This is located on one of the main streets of Central Falls that families identified as most convenient for them if they wanted to visit the resource and referral office. The phone line provides a single number that families can call to get assistance. The person staffing the phone speaks both English and Spanish. The role of this staff person is to connect the family with the resource they need or with someone who can provide such support.

The computerized service directory/databank is provided in hard copy and on disk to all key agencies. It will be updated quarterly to ensure that it remains current. The databank is also being set up on a website.

The team developed a refrigerator magnet in both English and Spanish telling how to call the resource and referral line. The team is using staff of the participating agencies to provide these magnets and related information on this resource to all parents of children in Central Falls early childhood programs. This is being done either via meetings with parents or through one-to-one contacts.

The goals were to ensure that (1) all agency staff and families have equal access to a common set of information and (2) families have access to this information either via a key community agency (e.g., the agency with which they are already involved) or via a call to the resource and referral line.

The team summarized its accomplishments by saying, "Together we were able to break down barriers to accessing services in our community. Because of our work, families will no longer have to experience several intake processes and tell their stories several times."

5. Resources—

- The Family Support Center operated through Children's Friend and Services is providing the office space, phone line, and staff for the resource and referral phone line and is maintaining the computerized service directory/databank.

- Staff hired by the Central Falls COZ entered data for the databank.

- The Early Care and Leadership Institute (funded via Head Start) provided funds for purchasing refrigerator magnets to advertise the databank, training staff regarding utilization of this resource and how to support families in accessing services, printing copies of the directory, and developing the website. The team summarized their plans in a document to use in approaching the Institute for support and to share with other key stakeholders in order to encourage their use of the directory and to encourage circulating directory information and refrigerator magnets to their families and staff. See "Central Falls Family Partnerships Directory Implementation Plan by the Central Falls Collaborative Planning Team" appearing at the end of this profile.

- One CPP team member is the Central Falls webmaster, and she provided direction related to the website.

- Many activities were carried out as part of the regular job roles of various CPP Team members. To this extent, personnel, facility, and operational support (e.g., mailings, office supplies) were provided on an in-kind basis by the team members.

6. Sustaining and Replicating (Carrying On After the CPP Facilitator Leaves)—After the last meeting at which the CPP team facilitator was present in June 2000, the team committed to working together in order to fully implement their action plan for the "single stop" resource and referral phone line along with a computerized service directory/databank. Now that the directory is in place, the team is no longer meeting formally as a CPP team. However, CPP team members are being included in the district-wide Steering Council for the Central

Falls 21st Century Initiative. In this way, CPP team members have used their work together as a springboard for future collaborations in order to promote community agency and school district activities to ensure that they are comprehensive and nonduplicative.

7. Lessons Learned in Relation to the CPP Model—

- *Shared leadership commitment*—It is critical to get key people involved and committed from the start. Its helps to ensure that this commitment makes it possible to reach the most people.

- *Facilitation*—It helped to have an outside facilitator who was neutral at the beginning and who encouraged the team to be realistic and to set concrete, attainable goals that were considered beneficial by team members both individually and collectively. Achieving this focus was critical to the team's accomplishments.

- *Team structure for collaboration*—Teams need to be patient at first. In the initial stages, it is very important to learn about each other as agencies, taking time to discuss the services offered by each and the potential opportunities and benefits of collaboration for individual agencies as well as the team/community as a whole. These discussions will assist the team in moving toward a clear understanding of each other and a clear and common goal. It is important to clarify expectations for team members, including time commitments, the length and frequency of meetings, and the basic time frame necessary to accomplish the team's initial goal(s).

  It is also important to establish a small core group to direct team efforts. A smaller group makes meetings more productive. Others can be involved later on a contributing/ad hoc basis or through stakeholder involvement strategies as noted below.

- *Stakeholder Involvement*—It is important that the team's action plan includes roles for all team members to play so that (1) all staff and related resources are fully utilized, (2) team members build buy-in through participation, and (3) no single partner is overburdened. It is also important that the team give attention to not only seeking the input of agency leadership, but also involve staff and families. For example, this team surveyed staff and family members to gather information needed to design a resource and referral mechanism that would be responsive to their needs. They also built in training for staff and families to make sure that this new resource would be properly used.

- *Visioning*—The team's vision: "Quality, inclusive, culturally competent and seamless early education and care services that are adequate in number and type to fully address the needs of children ages birth through six who are at risk and who have disabilities and their families."

  Lessons we have learned about visioning: Developing a shared vision helps to unify the team, providing the big picture (thinking big) from which smaller and more attainable goals can be established.

- *Priority setting (thinking big and starting small)*—The team identified the following priorities as challenges needing to be addressed to achieve the vision. Of these priorities, they decided to tackle priority item "a" first. Team members still hope to pursue the remaining priorities, either through the Steering Council for the Central Falls 21st Century Initiative or through some other means.

  a) Develop a mechanism to effectively and easily link families to the early care and education services through a databank of existing early education and care resources and a resource and referral line. This should include staff training about available services and skills they need to link families with these services. Resource and referral line usage will provide data about service gaps that can assist in community planning for comprehensive nonduplicative services.

b) Develop a community calendar and other strategies to coordinate existing services and agencies' activities in order to maximize limited resources and eliminate duplication.

c) Develop a common intake form for use across agencies.

d) Develop interagency strategies to ensure a smooth transition from one program/agency to another that is responsive to the needs of children, families, and the agencies that serve them.

Lessons we have learned about priority setting: It is very important to "think big and start small" with a clear and common focus and doable priorities.

- *Action Planning*—Action Planning helped to clarify expectations for team members and timelines. It broke the goal down into small, manageable steps.

- *Implementation of Action Plans*—Because the plan specified who needed to do what and when, people shared the workload and responsibility. It was important that this plan be a "living document" and not just a piece of paper filed away. Rather, the team reviewed the plan at their meetings, checking off tasks as they were accomplished. Sometimes, plans were revised as needed as the team learned new information. As each step was achieved, this helped the team see progress, providing momentum and boosting team morale.

- *Evaluation of Team Activities*—Data resulting from use of the "single stop" resource and referral phone line along with a computerized service directory/databank will be tracked on a monthly basis by the Family Support Center and shared semiannually with the Central Falls 21st Century Initiative. These data will assist in evaluating not only the resource and referral line and directory/databank but also in examining service needs as identified by families.

8. **Where Are They Now (Winter 2001–02)?** During the time of the project, collaboration increased as a result of team accomplishments. However, after a year or so, many of the team members changed jobs and/or agencies—particularly those that had played a leadership role on the team. This resulted in the team ending following the natural conclusion of the team's work/project.

Survey regarding Establishing a Central Falls Centralized Databank of Community Resources

Survey Overview: An interagency team of representatives from Early Intervention, Early Head Start, Head Start, the COZ, Central Falls Public Schools, Progreso Latino and the Heritage Park Day Care are investigating the need for Central Falls to have a Centralized Databank of Community Resources. This would be a place that people could visit or contact by phone or computer to find out what kinds of community resources are available to families of young children in Central Falls.

Instructions: Please answer the following questions so that we can have your ideas on the need for such a Databank and how it could best help families and staff from various agencies serving young children.

Are you responding as a family member? ___ Yes OR an agency staff member? ___ Yes

1. If there were a centralized place that could give you information on community resources, what kind of resources would you most want to know about?

____ medical services   ____ dental services
____ social services   ____ public school services
____ child care   ____ affordable housing
____ food   ____ clothing
____ transportation   ____ help with expenses
____ recreation   ____ legal services
____ counseling   ____ translations
____ respite care   ____ help for someone with a disability

Asked of part of the sample on some but not all surveys

____ after school tutoring programs   ____ security deposit and rental assistance
____ summer camps   ____ legal advocacy
____ father involvement   ____ youth services
____ domestic violence   ____ child support issues
____ utilities assistance (oil, light, gas) ____ continuing education
____ free trainings   ____ family support groups
____ financial assistance for private schools/scholarships
____ other (please tell us what that is)

2. What would be the most important things you would want to know about these resources?
___ agency name, address, phone   ___ specific name or title of a person to call
___ description of services they have   ___ any costs or fees involved
___ who is eligible for these services   ___ hours they are open
___ languages they speak and contact name for specific language
___ other (please tell us what that is)

3. How would you most like to be able to get this information?

    ___ over the phone   ___ in a brochure

    ___ in a written resource directory   ___ over a website on the computer

    ___ in a community office   ___ provided by a parent/professional

    ___ other (please tell us what that is)

4. Where could we locate this centralized place for information to make it easiest for you to get to (e.g., in the heart of town, on a general street with an ongoing bus line, etc.)?

5. Where do you usually go now when you are looking for information on community resources?

6. What other ideas do you have?

Central Falls Family Partnerships Directory Implementation Plan
by the Central Falls Collaborative Planning Team
June 1, 2000

What is the Central Falls Collaborative Planning Team?

We are a collaborative team of parents and professionals who are committed to working together in order to promote quality, inclusive, culturally competent, and seamless early education and care services that are adequate in number and type to fully address the needs of children ages birth through age six who are at risk and who have disabilities and their families. We represent:

- Captain Hunt School, Central Falls Public Schools

- Child Opportunity Zone, Central Falls Public Schools

- Early Head Start through Children's Friend and Service

- Early Intervention Services at Meeting Street Center

- Families of young children

- Head Start (Pawtucket/Central Falls Center)

- Progreso Latino

- Parents as Partners at Meeting Street Center

What is this directory that we propose?

- *A source of information*—This will be a centralized and computerized databank that provides information for family members and staff on services available to meet the needs of children ages birth through age six who are at risk and who have disabilities and their families. By September 2000, it will be available on a website that can be accessed by agencies and families, on a disk for key agencies in Central Falls (Partner Agencies), and in hard copy for Partner Agencies that do not yet have computers.

- *A source for referral to needed services*—

  1. A central directory contact will be available at the Family Support Center—a single number that families or agencies can call to get linked to services.

  2. Directories will also be located in Partner Agencies in Central Falls that have been identified through a survey of families and staff as the places they most frequently use to get information on community resources since these are places they already visit for services. Most of these agencies typically support families and others in locating services (e.g., their own clients who are using their services and sometimes others such a people calling for information, etc.). This databank will be a tool to help them carry out a function that they already have.

Why is this directory needed?

Families and staff in Central Falls need a mechanism to easily and effectively link families of young children to needed services. Agency staff are not aware of the array of early education and care services available in our community. As a result, families of young children are not knowledgeable about or linked to the array of services available in our community. Current directories, while very helpful, either have geographic limitations (e.g., Traveler's Aide is statewide) or the services included do not address the needs of families of young children adequately. Moreover, when current directories are made available, they do not always include making someone available to assist families and staff in accessing needed services listed in the directory. Finally, the directory's evaluation plan will yield data to assist the Central Falls Collaborative Planning Team in identifying service usage and gaps that can be addressed at some later point for planning purposes.

How will it operate?

Central Falls Family Partnerships Directory at the Family Support Center

- Directory "home" located at the Family Support Center at Children's Friend and Service on Dexter Street at 729-9179, maintain database on website and update as information becomes available—at least annually

- Provide hard copies and a disk of the directory to each of the Partner Agencies along with quarterly updates (at some future point, data can be "hot linked" via the Internet to Referring Agencies)

- Coordinate public awareness activities related to the directory's availability

- Maintain data on directory usage and design and conduct an annual evaluation of directory usage, compiling results and submitting to Central Falls Collaborative Planning Team

Partner Agencies

- Publicize directory's availability within respective agencies (e.g., providing directory "magnets" specifically developed for this purpose, written information, bulletin boards, parent meetings, and 1:1 conferences)

- Provide information to families and assist them in service linkage as appropriate (staff speak both English and Spanish)

- Maintain data on directory usage and provide annually to the directory's "home" at the Family Support Center for evaluation purposes

- Provide information to the directory's "home" on directory updates needed (as these are identified through use of the directory), such as new services to include and updates in current listings.

Cape Verdean Association	Central Falls Public Schools	Children's Friend and Service	Department of Children, Youth and Families	Head Start, Pawtucket/ Central Falls Center	Meeting Street	Progreso Latino	RI Parent Information Network	Visiting Nurses Association	YWCA
	• Captain Hunt School • COZ • Other services as appropriate	• Early Head Start • Family Support Center • Other services as appropriate			• Early Intervention Services • Parent to Parent • Other services as appropriate				

What information will be included in this directory?

- *Geographic area to be covered*—Central Falls, including regional and statewide services that are available to people in Central Falls

- *Directory format/services to be listed*—Those applicable to young children birth through age 6 and their families including:

    1. **An introduction explaining its use**

    2. **Municipal contact information**

    3. **Service descriptions** listed alphabetically by name of agency. These will include the following information on each service: agency name, address, phone: specific name or title of a person to call; description of services they have; any costs or fees involved including sliding scale, free and low-cost services; who is eligible for these services; hours they are open (including provision for flexible hours); languages they speak and contact name for specific language; how to access services; if they have home visits. No two services/agencies will be listed on the same page. This will make it easier to send out updates, making it possible to only send those pages that have changes without impacting page numbers.

    4. **Index** with an alphabetical listing of service types. Under each service type will be a listing of those agencies that provide that service so that the user can look up the service in the service descriptions. An agency that provides multiple services will be referenced every time that the types of services it provides are listed in the index. Types of services listed will include: adult education, GED and continuing education, training and internships; child care including after school care; child support issues; clothing; counseling (individual and family); computers (access to and training in for staff and families); disability services: domestic violence; drug rehabilitation; early childhood community programs for children under five; financial help with expenses; food; homeless shelters; housing—affordable housing and security deposit and rental assistance; legal services and advocacy; medical and dental services; parent involvement (both mother and father involvement); pregnancy screenings; public school services; recreation; respite care; sexually transmitted diseases information and free diagnostic clinics; social services; summer camps/programs; support groups for individuals and families; translations; transportation; utilities assistance (oil, light, gas); youth services (tutoring centers, sports centers, employment opportunities for young adults, activities particularly directed at 3:00–6:00 time frame)

How will this material be collected, updated, accessed, and made available in necessary languages?

1. *Initial Collection*—Using the Traveler's Aide Directory as our foundation, using services applicable to Central Falls, using the disk purchased from Traveler's Aide. Add nonduplicative services listed in the Parent to Parent Directory. Then, add nonduplicative services as recommended by staff at Progreso Latino, the Family Support Center at Children's Friend and Service, and Visiting Nurses Association. This data collection will be coordinated by Children's Friend and Service staff, and by COZ staff, utilizing Central Falls high school students and volunteers for data entry. A website will be set up for the directory with the assistance of the Special Education Teacher and Child Outreach Coordinator, Central Falls Public School.

2. *Updated*

    - Partner Agencies will provide updates to the "directory's home" on an ongoing basis, that is, as they become aware of new information or the inaccuracy of directory information. Updates can be transmitted via computer or, if needed, a form will be provided for this purpose.

    - On an annual basis, the Family Support Center will do a mailing to all agencies listed in the directory including at update form and return envelope. A mechanism will also be developed for updates to be transmitted via computer through the website. New data will be entered so that the website is up to date. Partner Agencies will be provided with updated information through their use of the website, or if needed/requested, updates will be sent to them in hard copy and/or on disk. The Family Support Center will use a variety of strategies for this update process, e.g., use of parents, volunteers, students, etc.

3. *Accessed/made available to people needing the information*

- Families and staff can access information through the website and through the disks and hard copies that will be made available to each Partner Agency. Even though the directory is on-line so that families can access it directly without agency help, Partner Agencies will continue to provide any current services that they may offer to support families in linking to services.

  Future possibility: At some point, training will be provided to families to help them use the website as independently as possible. They will also need to be made aware of where they can access computers so that they can use this resource independently. The directory will eventually also need to be translated—at least into Spanish.

- Training will be provided to Partner Agency staff on the directory's use via the Early Care and Leadership Institute to which the CPP team links.

- Means of publicizing the directory will include a refrigerator magnet in the shape of a house. The magnet will say:

> **Need help in locating services for young children and families?**
> **Contact: Family Support Center**
> **Necesita ayuda con servicios para niños y familias?**
> **Communiquese: Family Support Center**
> **729-0008 website: To be determined**

These will be provided to families and staff. These will be funded through the Early Care and Leadership Institute grant. Periodic public service announcements will also be made available through local media.

4. *Made available in necessary languages*—The team would identify which of the Partner Agencies can provide information on services (from the directory) in languages other than English. This information will be available by calling the Family Support Center and will be included in directory public awareness materials.

Where will this be housed?

The directory will be housed at the Family Support Center, Children's Friend and Service, Dexter Street. The responsibilities include those as outlined in this proposal. Costs incurred in being the "directory's home" are estimated to be $1000 annually for staff time, computer disks, printing, postage, and routine office supplies. These costs are over and above the routine resource and referral role that the Family Support Center already plays.

Cranston, RI, CPP Team Profile February–November 2000

1. **Team Description**—The Cranston, RI, CPP was a group of parents and professionals representing the agencies listed below and committed to increasing collaboration among agencies providing early education and care so that these services are seamless, inclusive, and adequate in quantity and quality to meet the needs of ALL children ages birth through kindergarten age (age six) and their families.

   During CPP participation, the team focused on (a) establishing a "Cranston Cabinet" of key agency decision-makers and (b) developing a universal release of information form.

2. **Partners**—In order to keep the team workable in size and scope, it was composed of individuals whose agency or interest was directly linked to the current focus of the team. These individuals were referred to as "regular members." The team also involved "contributing/ad hoc members" on an as-needed/consultative basis, having them meet with the team periodically when related to a relevant issue, seeking their input on key issues via a phone call, having a team member interview them, etc.

   ### Regular Members

   - Central Region Early Intervention
   - Comprehensive Community Action (includes Early Head Start and Head Start)
   - Cornerstone Preschool (Easter Seals of RI/Cranston ARC)
   - Cranston COZ (Child Opportunity Zone) Family Center (operated through the Cranston Public Schools)
   - Cranston Public Schools (preschool services, child outreach, special education services, and early intervention services)
   - Project READY (operated through the Cranston Public Schools)
   - Providence/Cranston Child Care Network
   - YMCA of Cranston, Kid's World

   ### Contributing/Ad Hoc Members

   - Family Member—Gladstone PTA President
   - Kid's Kingdom
   - Sunshine Preschool

3. **History and Development**—Although they had a history of collaborating from agency to agency, they had not collaborated as a communitywide team prior to becoming involved in the CPP. The CPP provided a mechanism to expand these existing collaborations into a formal comprehensive, collaborative, communitywide effort. The CPP facilitator worked with this team from February–November 2000 after which the team began operating on its own.

4. **Results**—The team targeted two challenges during the period of project participation facilitated by CPP staff. They produced these two accomplishments: (a) establishing a Cranston Cabinet and (b) developing a universal release of information form. The team's action plan related to these challenges appears at the end of this profile along with action plan direction for addressing their other challenges (which the team pursued on their own after the CPP facilitator left—see "Where Are They Now [Winter 2001–02]?" at the end of this profile).

   a) *Cranston Cabinet*—The "overarching" team priority was to establish a Cranston Cabinet structure to facilitate community planning associated with early childhood. Their Cranston Cabinet proposal is now in process with the public schools taking the lead on establishing this group over the coming year, not only for early childhood but to address issues related to children and youth of all ages.

      The Cranston Cabinet is a group of agency heads/"final" decision-makers. Membership models the state Children's Cabinet and includes the public school superintendent, comprehensive community action director, the mayor, the YMCA director, and other key agencies and officials either on a regular or ad hoc basis. Likely ad hoc members may include leadership from Central Region Early

Intervention, the police department, the library, mental health services, and CODAC. Individual cabinet members will be kept abreast of issues or recommendations to be presented to them by way of periodic communications from issue-specific teams or task groups as well as by way of individual team members from the cabinet members' agency. This cabinet will meet two to four times a year to:

- Establish interagency teams/committees of middle management and line staff, families, and others, as appropriate, to pursue particular community needs and/or respond to various initiatives that come down from state or federal levels (such as the CPP team);

- Provide input to these teams to help them set direction (such as providing input on the following four issues identified by the CPP team); and

- Serve as a source of final interagency decisions and commitment to support implementation of these decisions within their respective agencies.

b) *Universal Release of Information*—The team developed a universal release of information form acceptable to all agencies participating on the CPP team. The purpose of this form is to facilitate information sharing and planning among these agencies and to minimize paperwork duplication for families and agencies where children and families are either dually served and/or transitioning from one agency to another. This was completed in November 2000 and submitted to their respective agencies over the winter. Upon approval, the form was translated into the predominant languages of the Cranston community. Printing took place in the spring, being done by each participating agency on an agency need basis. Communitywide use began with the 2001–2002 year. Each agency was provided this form on computer disk and will assume responsibility for training staff and families within their agencies in its use. (The Release that was adopted and is now in use appears at the end of this profile.)

5. Resources—

- Many activities were carried out as part of the regular job roles of various CPP team members. To this extent, personnel, facility, and operational support (e.g., mailings, office supplies) were provided on an in-kind basis by the team members.

- Each agency will assume responsibility for (1) making copies of the universal release of information form that will be used within that agency and (2) training their staff in its use.

6. Sustaining and Replicating (Carrying On After the CPP Facilitator Leaves)—At the team's final meeting with the CPP team facilitator on November 15, 2000, the team committed to continuing its work, targeting the additional priorities it has set (see under item #7). They scheduled their next meeting for January 11, 2001 and made assignments for the facilitator and recorder for this session. At the January meeting, the team intends to:

a) Determine the manner in which it will address its three next priorities (e.g., one at a time, multiple priorities at one time);

b) Set its meeting schedule for the remainder of the school year (anticipating meeting every four to six weeks on a regular meeting schedule);

c) Identify a specific action plan for the priority(ies) that the team targets for next steps, taking into account its meeting schedule;

d) Identify who else may need to be involved with the team either as a regular or contributing/ad hoc member in light of the priority(ies) targeted;

e) Clarify team roles regarding co-chairs/facilitators, minutes, etc.; and

f) Finalize plans as needed for January 25, 2001 presentation.

7. Lessons Learned in Relation to the CPP Model—

- *Shared leadership commitment*—It is critical to have the key agencies all at the table and committed. This commitment served as the impetus to initiate meeting together to explore potential areas of collaboration.

- *Facilitation*—It helped to have an outside facilitator at the beginning who was knowledgeable about early childhood and about how to work with collaborative groups. This made it possible for the facilitator to share information on recommended practices and to be able to understand the issues with which the team was dealing. Having an outside facilitator at first meant that this person was neutral and the team trusted her to deal with everyone fairly.

  The facilitator served as a model for the team, increasing their awareness of the important issues such as having an agenda, staying focused and on task in meetings, having minutes to summarize discussion and decisions, and to clearly define next steps. Team participation also resulted in them learning a variety of facilitation processes such as visioning; how to assess community strengths, weaknesses, opportunities, and threats; how to do action planning as well as how to run meetings in general using processes such as open and round robin discussion, merging cards on a "sticky storyboard," flip chart, etc.

- *Team structure for collaboration*—It is important to keep the team manageable both in its size and its scope. Others can then be involved on an as-needed basis. It is also important to have shared responsibility for key team tasks, including convening and facilitating the sessions, taking and disseminating minutes, as well as carrying out the team's action plan.

- *Stakeholder Involvement*—It will be important as we move forward to keep people involved by choosing tasks that are meaningful to them and to the team as a whole.

- *Visioning*—The team's vision: "Increasing collaboration among agencies providing early education and care so that these services are seamless, inclusive, and adequate in quantity and quality to meet the needs of ALL children ages birth through kindergarten age (age six) and their families."

  Lessons we have learned about visioning: A vision helps the team focus its efforts. Developing a vision aided in building the "trust factor," helping the team establish common ground and a reason to work together in a way that would meet both individual and collective needs.

- *Priority setting (thinking big and starting small)*—The team established five priorities, tackling first: (a) establishing a Cranston Cabinet and (b) developing a universal release of information as described earlier in this profile. Additional priorities still to be addressed are presented below in the order in which they anticipate dealing with them:

a) Commonly adopted interagency policies, procedures, timelines, and forms related to the transition of children with and without special needs and their families from one agency to another (that is, among all agencies participating on the CPP team);

b) A computerized databank/website of services in Cranston for young children and their families to serve as a common information source for agencies and families in locating needed services. This databank would build on the Traveler's Aide directory and would be expanded to focus on Cranston and to include information on topics not currently addressed by Traveler's Aide (e.g., more detailed information on eligibility, more information on early childhood related topics, etc.); and

c) Personnel development strategies to ensure that agency staff and families have the knowledge and skills to support young children and to participate effectively in the process of transitioning from one Cranston early care and education agency to another.

Learnings about priority setting are: It is important to set priorities, selecting those that are doable. "Thinking big but starting small" results in tasks that, when achieved, help the team bond. These bonds serve as the foundation for continued collaborations.

- *Action Planning*—It is important to have a plan that clearly spells out what specific tasks need to be done by whom, when, etc.

- *Implementation of Action Plans*—The plan is the guide for the team's work—not a piece of paper to be set aside when done. As the team's guide, it helps keep the team on task and accountable. Of course, it can be adapted as needed in light of changing contexts and information learned during implementation.

- *Evaluation of Team Activities*—It is important for the team to routinely evaluate its work both formally and informally. The team plans to track the use of the universal release and evaluate its benefits and needed revisions.

8. **Where Are They Now (Winter 2001–02)?** The team has continued to meet. It has continued to work on the Cranston Cabinet and has fully implemented the universal release of information form. The team has worked with the Cranston family resource center known as a COZ (Child Opportunity Zone) to create a service directory for families with 50 pages of resource information. Current priorities are based on the vision initially established by the team and include (a) computerized service directory (available now to families and staff in hard copy); (b) commonly adopted interagency policies, procedures, timelines, and forms related to the transition of children with and without special needs and their families from one agency to another (among all agencies on CPP team); and (c) personnel development to ensure that staff and families have the knowledge and skills to support young children and to participate effectively in the process of transitioning from one Cranston early care and education agency to another.

Collaborative Planning Team Action Plan Form

Team: Cranston, RI   **Period Covered by Plan:** March 2000–June 2001

Vision: As a collaborative team representing Early Intervention, child care, Early Head Start, Head Start, and public schools, we are committed to increasing collaboration among agencies providing early education and care so that these services are seamless, inclusive, and adequate in quantity and quality to meet the needs of ALL children ages birth through kindergarten age (age six) and their families.

Challenge(s): Transition policies and procedures need to adopted on an interagency basis to clearly define roles, responsibilities, and timelines to provide for better communication among agencies. This process starts with universal home visiting to facilitate home-to-program transitions and extends through the early childhood transition points including, but not limited to, typical key early childhood transition point of children turning three years old and children transitioning into kindergarten services. The process will tap the COZ (Child Opportunity Zone) as a community clearinghouse of information, resources, and referrals for families and agencies to ensure that children and families do not fall through the cracks. The process needs to reconcile and integrate the different requirements under which each agency operates. It should facilitate information sharing on children/families in transition including general demographics as well as child/family-specific information to help in planning and supporting transitions. The transition process should address ALL children. It currently does not. It addresses children who have disabilities and who are eligible for Head Start. Even for this population, the process needs to be better articulated and more effective and efficient. It does not currently address "typical" children. It also does not address children who are at risk because of income, English as a Second Language, or other risk factors.

Objective	Strategies/ Action Steps	Resources	People	Timeline	Outcome
1A. Establish an interagency agreement related to transition policies and procedures to address ALL children ages birth through kindergarten to clearly define roles, responsibilities, and timelines to provide for better communication among agencies.	**NOTE:** The team has determined that Objective 1B (Universal Release of Information Form) and Objective 3 (Cranston Cabinet) are first priorities chronologically. After completion of work plans for 1B and 3, the team will tackle (in this order) 1A, 2, and 1C.				

Collaborative Planning Team Action Plan Form

Team: Cranston, RI   **Period Covered by Plan:** March 2000–June 2001

Vision: As a collaborative team representing Early Intervention, child care, Early Head Start, Head Start, and public schools, we are committed to increasing collaboration among agencies providing early education and care so that these services are seamless, inclusive, and adequate in quantity and quality to meet the needs of ALL children ages birth through kindergarten age (age six) and their families.

Challenge(s): The adoption of common forms supporting these interagency transition policies and procedures (e.g., use of a universal release of information form) would facilitate communication and make agency requests for information from parents and providers less duplicative.

Objective	Strategies/ Action Steps	Resources	People	Timeline	Outcome
1B. Adopt *common forms* supporting these policies and procedures (e.g., use of a universal release of information form) to facilitate communication and make agency requests for information from parents and providers less duplicative. **NOTE:** Other forms (in addition to the universal release of information form) will be developed as needed as part of the action plan for 1A (overall transition policies and procedures).	1B.1. Obtain: • Existing releases from each agency. • Forms from other states. We already have VA form and direction from RI. • Information on what is legally required from a state/federal perspective and through local agency policies and procedures.	• Agency releases. • Releases from other states. • RI Interagency TA Guide legal side-by-side for state/fed. • Local agency policies. • State EI/DOH policy person.	• ALL Team members. • COZ.	Homework prior to 9/14 meeting: Locate and bring 12 copies to the meeting.	At 9/14 meeting, forms obtained for: At 9/14 meeting, legal requirements obtained for:

Objective	Strategies/ Action Steps	Resources	People	Timeline	Outcome
1B. (continued) Adopt *common forms* supporting these policies and procedures (e.g., use of a universal release of information form) to facilitate communication and make agency requests for information from parents and providers less duplicative.	1B.2. Meeting agenda: • Review agency forms regarding commonalities and differences; identify features we like/don't like. • Define types of information we want/need to share and why (for which release will be used). • Identify form parameters (legal requirements impacting the form, essential items vs. non-essential items, how long form is good for, etc.). • Design or select/adapt a rough draft of a common template that can be shared electronically.	Parent input via advisory board representatives attending our 9/14 meeting.	Team members, facilitated by Dennis, will invite a parent representative from their respective agency advisory groups: Cranston Special Education Advisory Committee, Project READY Advisory Committee, Head Start Policy Council, other advisory committees as appropriate.	9/14 Team Meeting, Noon–3:00, Project READY Office at Gladstone Elementary. *(It may be necessary to spread these tasks over two meetings.)*	9/14 Team Meeting Outcomes:

Objective	Strategies/Action Steps	Resources	People	Timeline	Outcome
1B. (continued) Adopt *common forms* supporting these policies and procedures (e.g., use of a universal release of information form) to facilitate communication and make agency requests for information from parents and providers less duplicative.	1B.3. Circulate draft form for comment.	Get input from Cranston Cabinet and other individuals/entities as appropriate.	To be determined.	Within one month of form completion.	Feedback received on form:
	1B.4. • Revise form as needed based on input received. • Make plans to resubmit form as needed to Cranston Cabinet and to get state officials' okay. • Identify types of people who will most typically use form. Design strategies to provide them with information/training. • Develop feedback mechanism regarding form so that form and procedures for its use can be revised as needed.			Team meeting, date to be determined, Noon–3:00, Cranston Head Start (this is the last meeting facilitated by Peggy Hayden, CPP staff).	Meeting outcomes:

Objective	Strategies/ Action Steps	Resources	People	Timeline	Outcome
1B. (continued) Adopt *common forms* supporting these policies and procedures (e.g., use of a universal release of information form) to facilitate communication and make agency requests for information from parents and providers less duplicative.	1B.5. Implement form use, training, etc. per plans developed at previous meeting.		Upon adoption of form.	Individual agencies via CPP team leadership.	Record of events regarding form training and dissemination activities:
	1B.6. Evaluate whether or not the team accomplished its objective, revising form and procedures for use as needed.		To be determined.	CPP team Meeting.	Evaluation of Objective:

Collaborative Planning Team Action Plan Form

Team: Cranston, RI   **Period Covered by Plan:** March 2000–June 2001

Vision: As a collaborative team representing Early Intervention, child care, Early Head Start, Head Start, and public schools, we are committed to increasing collaboration among agencies providing early education and care so that these services are seamless, inclusive, and adequate in quantity and quality to meet the needs of ALL children ages birth through kindergarten age (age six) and their families.

Challenge(s): In order for a communitywide transition process to be effective, staff and families involved in this process must have the necessary knowledge and skills to participate effectively in the process and ensure program continuity as children and families move from one program to another.

Objective	Strategies/ Action Steps	Resources	People	Timeline	Outcome
1C. Develop and implement a *collaborative personnel development plan* to ensure that *staff and families* involved in the transition process *have the necessary knowledge and skills* to participate effectively in the process and to ensure program continuity as children and families move from one program to another. **NOTE:** The action plan for this objective will be developed later, potentially Spring 2001 or 2001–2002. Initial ideas generated by the team in Spring 2000 are presented on the plan form here.	1C.1. Common agreement on what "transition" is so that everyone will have a common understanding.		• Project READY.		
	1C.2. Common agreement on what "ready to learn" is.		• Project READY.		
	1C.3. Education campaign to help people realize what is available.		• K teachers. • Parents of kids at home; all parents. • Preschool. • Technical assistance to preschools.		

Objective	Strategies/ Action Steps	Resources	People	Timeline	Outcome
1C. Develop and implement a *collaborative personnel development plan* to ensure that *staff and families* involved in the transition process *have the necessary knowledge and skills* to participate effectively in the process and to ensure program continuity as children and families move from one program to another. **NOTE:** The action plan for this objective will be developed later, potentially Spring 2001 or 2001–2002. Initial ideas generated by the team in Spring 2000 are presented on the plan form here.	1C.4. Address needs of those people not serviced.		• Pediatricians. • Librarians. • Supermarket. • Laundromats. • Heath centers. • Churches. • Ethnic societies. • Cambodian. Society. • Private schools. • Portuguese Club, etc.		
	1C.5. Determine who should or should not be in kindergarten—do we meet the child where he or she is or do we send him or her back home or to preschool?		• Cranston Public School Administration		

Collaborative Planning Team Action Plan Form

Team: Cranston, RI   **Period Covered by Plan:** March 2000–June 2001

Vision: As a collaborative team representing Early Intervention, child care, Early Head Start, Head Start, and public schools, we are committed to increasing collaboration among agencies providing early education and care so that these services are seamless, inclusive, and adequate in quantity and quality to meet the needs of ALL children ages birth through kindergarten age (age six) and their families.

Challenge(s): There is a **lack of services for children who are at risk**; that is, no services for them to "transition from or to." These are children who are at risk because of income, English as a Second Language, or other risk factors and who do not qualify for existing services (early intervention, special education, Early Head Start, and Head Start). They need a comprehensive, inclusive quality program that includes language enrichment opportunities. Increasingly, welfare-to-work programs are resulting in families that were previously eligible for Head Start that no longer meet income guidelines. Although Head Start can waive these guidelines, it can do so only for 10% of its enrollment. Sometimes, even when children qualify for Head Start, slots may not always be available for them. Each agency individually and the community in general currently has resource limitations (time, money, and space) that impede the ability to address service needs in the community. The absence of such programs increases that likelihood that these children may be identified as needing special education during the primary school years.

Objective	Strategies/Action Steps	Resources	People	Timeline	Outcome
2. Develop an interagency plan to *expand services for children who are at risk*, creating a collaborative multi-agency program which braids together a variety of current and new funding streams to provide comprehensive, inclusive quality services.	**NOTE:** The team has decided to approach this objective by first developing an action plan to assess what services are currently available through the development of a computerized data-bank/website of services in Cranston for young children and their families to serve as a common information source for agencies and families in locating needed services.				

Objective	Strategies/ Action Steps	Resources	People	Timeline	Outcome
2. (continued) Develop an interagency plan to *expand services for children who are at risk,* creating a collaborative multi-agency program which braids together a variety of current and new funding streams to provide comprehensive, inclusive quality services.	This databank would build on the Traveler's Aide directory and would be expanded to focus on Cranston and to include information on topics not currently addressed by Traveler's Aide (e.g., more detailed information on eligibility, more information on early childhood related topics, etc.). This action plan will be developed at some future date, likely in Spring 2001 or during the 2001–2002 school year.				

Collaborative Planning Team Action Plan Form

Team: Cranston, RI   **Period Covered by Plan:** March 2000–June 2001

Vision: As a collaborative team representing Early Intervention, child care, Early Head Start, Head Start, and public schools, we are committed to increasing collaboration among agencies providing early education and care so that these services are seamless, inclusive, and adequate in quantity and quality to meet the needs of ALL children ages birth through kindergarten age (age six) and their families.

Challenge(s): Along with these service gaps, existing services are fragmented and sometimes duplicative. There is a need for a communitywide mechanism to coordinate early childhood services and to address these issues. However, there is no "central" coordinating group that brings together "final" decision-makers. Rather, there are now numerous topic-specific coordinating groups related to early childhood with similar agendas and frequently involving essentially the same agencies/staff. All key players need to be involved in relevant coordinating groups if these groups are to be truly effective. The group needs to be effective to the extent that it can "stand the test of time, transcending people currently in place."

Objective	Strategies/Action Steps	Resources	People	Timeline	Outcome
3. Establish a **Cranston Cabinet** to create a **community-wide mechanism to coordinate early childhood services** and to address issues of service gaps, duplication, and fragmentation. This central coordinating cabinet will bring together "final" decision-makers and involve middle management, line staff, and families as appropriate in committees addressing topical issues.	3.1. Focus of collaboration is a shared vision, shared resources, and shared problems. 3.2. Identify participants who are able to commit resources. 3.2a. Use personal contact to engage the agency. 3.3. Establish a leadership structure.	Established agencies in the community.	• Superintendent of Schools. • CCAP Director. • YMCA Director. • City of Cranston. • MHS Director. • Chief of Police. • CODAC Director. • Libraries Director.	March 2000–June 2001	June 1, 2000 Status: 1. The team developed a proposal for a Cranston Cabinet at its 4/27 session and submitted to agency decision-makers. 2. As of 6/1, decision-maker input from the public schools and early intervention supports proceeding with this proposal. 3. Peggy Hayden will secure a copy of the state level Children's Cabinet membership list to serve as a resource for pursuing this proposal. She will send this to Dennis.

Objective	Strategies/ Action Steps	Resources	People	Timeline	Outcome
3. (continued) Establish a **Cranston Cabinet** to create a **communitywide mechanism to coordinate early childhood services** and to address issues of service gaps, duplication, and fragmentation. This central coordinating cabinet will bring together "final" decision-makers and involve middle management, line staff, and families as appropriate in committees addressing topical issues.	3.4 Establish a "point person" to facilitate the work of the cabinet. 3.5 The cabinet will have established subcommittees comprised of representatives designated by cabinet members. 3.6 The cabinet will act as a clearinghouse for information and funding opportunities.		• Senior Services Director. • DHS. • DCYF. • Department of Education.		4. During July 2000, Dennis will convene a meeting with Peggy Hayden and the Project READY consultant to plan a meeting of agency decision-makers at which they decide regarding proceeding with this proposal. CPP team comments in this regard: • Cranston Cabinet is a LOCAL group who link to state counterparts as needed. • Intent is that this is a meeting of decision-makers. If they send designees, these should have the power to decide. • Cabinet focus should be narrow enough so members have much in common and will find meetings relevant and thus be likely to attend. Others whose involvement would be more "issue specific" can be involved on an as-needed basis.

Objective	Strategies/ Action Steps	Resources	People	Timeline	Outcome
3. Establish a **Cranston Cabinet** to create a **community-wide mechanism to coordinate early childhood services** and to address issues of service gaps, duplication, and fragmentation. This central coordinating cabinet will bring together "final" decision-makers and involve middle management, line staff, and families as appropriate in committees addressing topical issues.					5. A meeting of decision-makers will be held (hopefully prior to CPP team's 9/14 meeting) to determine direction. Likely participants would be: Charlie (facilitator), Catherine, Jim, Carol, Ernie, Joanne, Robert.

Cranston Collaboration Universal Release of Information Procedures

Who will use this release? Staff and parent representatives from these agencies/programs developed the following release for their use:

- Comprehensive Community Action, which includes Early Head Start and Head Start
- Cornerstone Preschool (Easter Seals of RI/Cranston ARC)
- Cranston COZ Family Center (operated through the Cranston Public Schools)
- Cranston Public Schools (preschool services, child outreach, special education services, and early intervention services)
- Cranston Region Early Intervention
- Project READY (operated through the Cranston Public Schools)
- YMCA of Cranston, Kid's World
- Others as appropriate

What is its purpose and how can this purpose be fulfilled using this release? To facilitate information sharing and planning among these agencies/programs and to minimize paperwork duplication for families and agencies where children and families are either dually served and/or transitioning from one agency/program to another. To fulfill this purpose, as long as it is appropriate to the circumstances at hand, agencies will:

- When feasible, use one release to share information among multiple agencies. If this is the case, all relevant agencies should be listed at the top of the release in the space for "agency(ies)." There may be instances where records checked for release will be shared with some but not all agencies listed at the top of the release. To accommodate this, make an appropriate notation in the space after the type of record checked, e.g., "applies only to names of agencies" or "applies to all agencies listed above";
- Use general terminology in the release Purpose section to allow flexibility in information sharing. e.g., "to assist with the identification, location, evaluation,

and/or placement of the child," "for educational planning," etc.; and
- Specify one year as the time period for which the authorization will be valid.

How will it be made available for use? It will be provided on disk to all participating agencies. It will be provided in English and the other predominant languages in Cranston as identified by the ESL Office, Cranston School Department. Agencies will individually assume responsibility for release printing and distribution as appropriate to each agency's circumstances and resources, e.g., paper copies, on agency websites, etc. It is suggested that agencies consider having a notation on the bottom of the release to indicate who gets copies of the release. Each agency will be responsible for training its own staff regarding release use and related confidentiality policies and procedures.

How does this release comply with requirements of each individual agency/program? The release was developed through a team representing the agencies/programs that will use it. Therefore, it is assumed to meet "core" requirements for these agencies. It is also understood that the use of this "common" release does not supersede any individual agency requirements associated with confidentiality. That is, all individual agency requirements still stand.

Can an individual agency add items to this release? It is agreed that agencies can add items as needed to this release. It is assumed that such additions will be minor and few in number. That is, in adding items, agencies should remember to keep the release as similar to the original as possible to fulfill the purposes for which the release was developed.

When will agencies being using this release? Beginning with the 2001–02 school year.

Cranston Collaboration Universal Release of Information

I hereby authorize _____ to (check any of the three

items below that apply):   ___ Release To   ___ Obtain From   ___ Verbally Exchange With

Agency(ies): _____

_____

the following information regarding my child:

Name: _____ Date of Birth: _____

Address: _____

Child's Current School/Program: _____

Check all records to which this release applies:

___ Psychological Evaluation _____

___ Educational Evaluation _____

___ Social History Evaluation _____

___ Individual Education Plan (IEP) _____

___ Speech/Language Evaluation _____

___ Psychiatric Evaluation _____

___ Health/Medical Evaluation _____

___ Other _____

___ Other _____

Purpose: _____

_____

I understand that these records are protected under the legal requirements under Federal
Confidentiality Regulations (42 CFR Part 2) and these state requirements:

_____ RI Law 78H-7522   _____ RI Law 40.1-2-26   _____ RI Law 5.37.3-4.

These records cannot be disclosed, given, sold, transferred, or in any way relayed to any other person not specified in this release. This consent for release can be withdrawn in writing at any time.

This authorization is valid from _____ until _____
(specify date, event, or condition upon which this release of information expires)

_____   _____   _____

Signature   Relationship   Date

_____   _____

Witness   Date

REDISCLOSURE PROHIBITED: *This information has been disclosed to you from records whose confidentiality is
protected by Federal Law. Federal Regulations (42 CFR Part 2) prohibit you from making any further disclosures
of it without the specific written consent of the person to whom it pertains or as otherwise permitted by such regulations. A general authorization for the release of medical or other information is not sufficient for this purpose.*

Denver, CO, CPP Team Profile 1998–2000

1. **Team Description**—The Denver, CO, CPP Team was an interagency team of parents and early childhood leaders who committed to meeting together for a year "to make the early childhood system(s) in Denver work better; starting with service coordination, IFSP development, child identification, and referrals."

   During CPP participation, the team focused on issues pertaining to infants and toddlers with special needs and their families under Part C of the Individuals with Disabilities Education Act (IDEA) with particular emphasis on service coordination.

2. **Partners**—The core team was made up of local stakeholders, but their equivalent state agencies sent representatives to key meetings and received copies of all minutes to stay informed. The team of representatives included (see the following chart):

3. **History and Development**—The kickoff event for this extensive collaborative effort was a "Town Hall" type gathering in October of 1998 with 40 direct service providers and parents from the city of Denver. Sponsored by the Community Action Resource Team from Denver Early Childhood Connections (Part C Organization), the event was called "C.A.R.T.ography—Mapping Our Journey." The planning group asked the CPP facilitator to help plan this day-long retreat and to use it as a community needs assessment and foundation for future collaborative efforts as an outreach site for the Collaborative Planning Project. This was also seen as a first step in building better interagency relations between several agencies that had experienced tremendous upheaval and turmoil in the past.

   After a morning of hearing stories of successful collaborative efforts in other Colorado Part C communities, the providers and parents split into small groups to identify the most relevant local issues and concerns. They didn't leave until strategies and next steps were clearly mapped out. Despite a long day of hard

Local Stakeholders	State Stakeholders
Denver Public Schools (DPS)	Colorado Department of Education
Denver Early Childhood Connections (Part C)	Colorado Department of Education
Sewall Child Development Center	Colorado Department of Education
Denver Options (DD system)	Colorado Department of Human Resources
Denver Social Services	Colorado Department of Human Resources
Denver Health	Colorado Department of Health Care Financing
NICU Consortium (neonatal intensive care units from area hospitals)	The Children's Hospital
Parents of young children with special needs	JFK Partners (JAP)

work, participants left feeling energized and renewed in their commitment to find better ways of working together as a community.

Each participant signed up to be part of a volunteer action team with the issue/strategy they were most concerned about.

C.A.R.T.ography—Mapping Our Journey
A Community Needs Assessment

Issue/Concern	Strategies/Next Steps
Identification and Eligibility • Lack of concern for parental involvement. • Need to deal with time/process barriers for categorically eligible children.	• Build relationships during home visits. • Provide training from parent perspective. • After initial referral, clarify minimum information needed to proceed and communicate with all parties.
Service Coordination • Confusion! Too many players. • Clarify roles and responsibilities for each service coordinator.	• Players need to define roles and how they overlap. • Clarify process from first contact.
IFSP • Lack of fluidity in process, and forms that do not reflect change. • Too many different forms.	• Come to consensus about process and create consistency about process regardless of entry point. • Collaboration between families and agencies to create a uniform form.
Transition • Kids falling thru cracks: not enough information shared. • Confusion and inconsistency regarding rules.	• Identify cracks/gaps and those kids. • Create task force with timelines—write down what each agency does, educate community resource providers.

A small planning team gathered to identify key stakeholders to work on these same issues from administrative and decision-making levels. The challenge was to not only find a good day for all these very committed people to meet, but to entice them to come together and work collaboratively after a recent series of very difficult interagency experiences. There was also a feeling that local systems change efforts could not happen without strong state support. A solution was discovered for both challenges by inviting equivalent state agency representatives for each local representative. Because the state capitol of Colorado is in Denver and because of the recent difficulties in interagency cooperation, people from the state agencies were available and interested in attending. Knowing that the state agencies

were aware and involved, the local stakeholders felt more supported and able to commit their time and energy.

The group began by examining the difficult issues with previous interagency relationships. In the mid '80's, some of the same participants had worked together to shape a system for infants, toddlers and their families that looked like a funnel. The theory was that children come into the system in many ways, but they should all be directed to Child Find for intake, evaluation, and referrals. The team of stakeholders realized that over the years, the "funnel" had evolved into a "colander"! Young children and families were falling through the holes of the system and experiencing diverse levels of quality and different kinds of access to resources.

The team decided to commit to improving the overall system in the four areas already identified by direct service providers. State agencies would stay in touch with the local efforts by reviewing minutes of each meeting and by having one member of the state Part C/Memo of Understanding Interagency Group who offered to serve as a liaison. The team came up with the following operating procedures:

Ground Rules

- All participants will have an equal voice.

- Minutes of all meetings will be recorded and shared with relevant state agencies.

- All stakeholders will bring information back to our own community.

- Make decisions by consensus.

- Indicate information intended for group only (confidentiality).

- Be respectful.

- Don't bash one system over another.

The team then met monthly over the course of a year. The CPP facilitator worked with them for the first six months. A facilitator was hired for the remaining time, because all members of the team wanted to fully participate in the meetings. Three different parents attended the first few meetings and shared their family story. Each story added greatly to the sessions, adding momentum and a good dose of reality when needed.

The Volunteer Action Teams from the C.A.R.T.ography retreat reported progress to the core team. The core team reprioritized their work based on the Action Team's recommendations. The primary focus chosen by the team was service coordination.

4. Results—

- *IFSP Development:* The Action Team gathered numerous IFSP forms from different agencies and different communities. They took the best from each and created a new form. The committee proposed that agencies use one form to prevent families from having to fill out multiple IFSP forms.

- *Shared consent form:* The team developed a shared consent form to be used by all agencies.

- *Transition:* The Action Team outlined issues needing interagency planning and written agreements (MOUs) and identified technical assistance through a series of forums explaining transition processes for families. Their continued goal was to ensure continuity of services for young children regardless of what time of year they are born.

- *Identification and Eligibility:* The Action Team wrote a grant to build greater community capacity for timely eligibility and evaluation through play-based assessments. Community-based practitioners could learn how to conduct play-based assessments in exchange for their volunteer services, in an attempt to reduce waiting times for families with young children. DPS is also discussing alternatives to increase capacity for evaluation and reduce waiting time for families.

- *Service Coordination:* This Action Team used the JFK Partners' guidebook on "Successful Community Collaboration" and the Colorado Department of Education's "Colorado Guidelines for Service Coordination" to develop a survey-questionnaire that was given to service coordinators to find out what they do and how they do it. Data from the survey was used to help analyze "the big picture" of service coordination in Denver.

- *Interagency Memorandum of Understanding for Part C Service Coordination:* Developed by and for the following agencies:

  - Denver Public Schools Child Find
  - Denver Health Children and Families Program
  - Denver Early Childhood Connections (Part C)
  - Denver Options (Community Center Board)

"The purpose of the agreement is to delineate a system of service coordination for families in Denver County having a child potentially eligible for Part C services. This agreement is designed to assure that all eligible families receive the same information, assurances, and options regardless of which agency provides service coordination and that each family is provided with one service coordinator." The process for families and service coordinators is clearly defined in the agreement. Gathering consensus and signatures to this written interagency agreement took several months and a lot of dedication by all participants. (A copy of this agreement, known as the "Interagency Community Partnership for Part C Services Coordination in Denver County," appears at the end of this profile.)

5. Resources—Denver Early Childhood Connections provided a consistent meeting place and resources to hire an outside facilitator for team meetings after the CPP facilitator had left. All agencies provided "in kind" time of personnel to participate in monthly half-day meetings. The Colorado Department of Education representative acted as a liaison between the local and the state organizations and the Part C Memo of Understanding Committee. Many people volunteered extra time and energy and dedication.

6. Sustaining and Replicating (Carrying On After the CPP Facilitator Leaves)—The team quickly decided to hire an outside facilitator after the first six months of CPP project facilitation. Each member wanted to fully participate in meetings rather than take on the role of facilitator. The goals were originally developed by people who know day-to-day issues—the direct service providers and families. The systems change team—made up of decision-makers and administrators—felt empowered to work on the meaningful and practical goals developed in the community. The local team felt support from the state level. All of these factors combined to sustain the effort for this community with a shared vision.

7. Lessons Learned in Relation to the CPP Model—

- *The importance of state support for local issues!* The fact that state agency representatives attended meetings (especially the first one) and received copies of meeting minutes provided support to local team members. During systems change efforts and uncertain times, it's great to have the "blessing" of higher administration. The local team was given permission to take time to identify concerns and work out strategies.

- *The importance of support from direct service providers and families!* The community's town hall kickoff event produced not only clear-cut goals and objectives but also teams of volunteers ready to work on specific activities for each goal. This broad-based foundational support provided momentum and impetus to the local planning team. They were grounded in reality rather than theory.

- *The importance of people to be willing to forgive and forget past troubles and move forward together in a collaborative manner.* Members of the planning team were willing to come together and try to renew troubled relationships. Ground rules made the meetings a "safe" place where they could openly discuss difficult issues. They realized that they shared a common vision and that everyone wanted to improve quality of services for young children and their families. When times got tough during the course of the year, team members could always renew momentum by remembering the shared purpose and why they were meeting in the first place.

- *Systems change doesn't happen in one electrical moment—seemingly small changes also impact people and systems!* After one meeting, the health representative started attending the interagency intake and referral meetings. The monthly meetings provided consistent times for different members to connect and receive feedback about the quality of services provided. Instead of waiting until the end of the project to make the systems change, these small systems change pieces continued to happen throughout the year.

8. Where Are They Now (Winter 2001–02)? The CPP team/Part C team has evolved from not being able to agree on how to start with referrals to having written interagency agreements and organized TA on service coordination. Partnerships, relationships, and collaborative activities among agencies have improved almost 100%. They started with agencies who had a very difficult conflict-filled history. During CPP, they were able to find a shared vision for infants, toddlers, and families in their community. Today, they have joint staff meetings, are planning trainings on transdisciplinary methods, and are discussing the need for a computer person to link databases among agencies. Early interventionists are working collaboratively with school district staff to assess children, to plan for families on the waiting lists, to ease transitions, and to provide jointly staffed home visits. They have also impacted the state system. That is, during CPP, they identified service coordination and its lack of coordination as the team's biggest challenge. They communicated that to the state, which responded by dedicating resources to statewide training/TA for core competencies on service coordination, rewriting state guidelines for using family resources and insurance, and working closely with the Denver team to create an understanding of funding streams and a hierarchy for using different resources.

Interagency Community Partnership for Part C Services Coordination in Denver County

I. Time Period Covered by This Agreement

This agreement will begin on _____, 2000 and will be reviewed and amended as needed in six months. The Service Coordination committee made up of representatives from Denver Public Schools (DPS) Child Find, Denver Health Children and Families Program, Denver Early Childhood Connections, Denver Options, and at least two family representatives will conduct the review and evaluation of the process.

II. Agencies Affected Include, But Are Not Limited to:

- Denver Public Schools (DPS) Child Find
- Denver Health Children and Families Program (DHCP)
- Denver Early Childhood Connections (DECC)
- Denver Options

III. Purpose

The purpose of this agreement is to delineate a system of service coordination for families in Denver County having a child potentially eligible for Part C services. This agreement is designed to assure that all eligible families receive the same information, assurances, and options regardless of which agency provides service coordination and that each family is provided with one service coordinator.

IV. Agreements

The above mentioned agencies share a common vision of providing meaningful supports and services in natural environments (to the extent desired by families) to families who have a young child with developmental delays in Denver. The following are statements of agreement.

1. A service coordinator from DECC will be assigned as soon as possible after referral of potentially eligible children to any of the participating agencies (not over five working days).

2. The referring agency will share coded information with the central data manager who will check for duplication prior to assigning a service coordinator (if the family is already connected with another agency, they are referred back to that agency). The data manager will keep a log of calls for all new referrals. The service coordinator will work in collaboration with the referring agency to best support the family.

3. The service coordinator will contact the family prior to a multidisciplinary assessment, and assure that the family receives a parent education about their rights, a referral to Child Find, and coaching about the parent's role during an IFSP. The service coordinator will also gather information such as priorities, concerns, and resources from the family to aid in planning the multidisciplinary assessment and in the development of the IFSP.

4. Prior to the IFSP, the service coordinator will assist the family in finding supports and services to meet their basic needs including immediate health and medical issues, housing, transportation, and other prioritized needs.

5. The service coordinator will negotiate with the other significant providers to be clear about respective roles and responsibilities with regard to service coordination functions.

6. After a child is determined to be eligible for Part C and the family requests paid services, they will be referred to Denver Options.

7. Families will be referred to DHCP when they fit their protocols for services.

8. Families may request a different service coordinator.

9. The roles and responsibilities of a service coordinator are based on IDEA Part C, the CICC Core Competencies and *Colorado Guidelines for Service Coordination*.

10. All signers or their representatives of this document agree to participate in the evaluation of the Denver process, IFSP monitoring and CART committees.

11. As other entities take on the role of service coordinator they will be asked to agree to and sign off on the specifics of this community partnership agreement.

    • Training: The Lead Service Coordinator, in conjunction with the participating agencies, will assess the training needs of the community through the CART committees. A training plan will be developed with training sessions occurring across the Denver community on a regular basis. All service coordinators are expected to attend the core competency training offered by CDE.

    • Evaluation of the service coordination system will be an interagency task performed on a bi-annual basis beginning six months after the signing of this agreement. Evaluation protocols will be developed as an interagency task to assess the quality of service coordination. A review team will meet monthly to review at least 10% of the IFSPs developed that month. The annual training plan will address training needs identified in this process.

V. Process

The signers of this agreement will, with the family's permission, refer families of potentially eligible children seeking information and/or services for infants and toddlers, birth to age three, to Denver Early Childhood Connections (DECC). When a referral is made to any of the participating agencies the process below will be followed with each agency taking responsibility for their roles as defined.

DECC will:

1. Assign a service coordinator within two working days of contact.

2. Check for duplication to determine if the child/family is currently receiving services from another agency, then collaborate with other agencies who may be involved to best support the needs of the family and child.

3. Contact the family within five working days to schedule a home visit* at which time the service coordinator will:

   • Explain to the family procedural safeguards and their rights under Part C of IDEA.

   • Ask the family to sign the Denver Interagency Consent Form and other needed consent forms to obtain pertinent records in determining the child's eligibility.

   • Discuss with the family their concerns, needs, priorities, and resources.

   • Assist the family as needed to address any emergent needs, concerns, or priorities such as housing, financial services, social services referral, transportation, etc.

   • Share information with the family about community resources, the "Denver Process," and natural environments (ERAP—Everyday Routines Activities and Places).

   • Procure records of prior assessments, or medical information pertinent to eligibility or needed in planning supports and services.

4. Notify Child Find of the referral so that a Child Find case manager can be assigned to coordinate further evaluation and for data collection.

5. Coordinate completion of the levels of development on the IFSP for children who do not need or consent to a multi-disciplinary assessment by Child Find.

6. Participate in the development of the IFSP.

7. Maintain contact with the family for parent to parent support, parent education/leadership opportunities, newsletter distribution, and dispute resolution.

8. Assist the family in transitioning to a service coordinator from Denver Options when receiving Denver Options paid services (including those referred for Family Support only).

9. Maintain the Denver County database for federal reporting.

10. Use information from the database to plan for needs of the community

*(Home visits may occur at home, the hospital, or another site of the family's choosing but are still referred to as "home visits.")

The Child Find Team will:

1. Complete a referral by having the Child Find liaison:

   - Complete the family intake data information and explain to the family the interagency process.

   - Contact Denver Early Childhood Connections to receive the assignment of a service coordinator.

   - Send to the family an information pamphlet that explains the interagency process and includes the names of the service coordinator, community contact people, and important community telephone numbers.

2. Collaborate with the service coordinator in scheduling the evaluation, attending the evaluation, writing the IFSP, supporting the family during the evaluation and IFSP process, and assisting the family with transportation, if necessary.

3. The Child Find team, service coordinator, and the family will complete the evaluation and develop the IFSP with recommendations for services and supports.

4. In collaboration with the service coordinator, present the child at IRT for review of service needs, resources, family priorities and family options. (The IRT process will allow for paperwork exchange, acknowledgment of services available, acknowledgment of family supports, and suggestions for community supports).

5. The Child Find case manager will complete all paperwork, submit the paperwork for processing, and close the case.

When a referral is made to Denver Options for paid services, they will become the service coordinator to ensure that funding for services will be available and the child will received the recommended services and supports.

Denver Options will:

1. Refer all families who call Denver Options for paid services to DECC for service coordination.

2. Receive referrals at IRT and assign a service coordinator within three working days. Child Find, DECC, and DHCP will be notified of the assignment at the following IRT meeting.

3. Not assign a service coordinator when there is a waiting list and will place the child's name on the waiting list. Child will receive funding on a first come, first served basis.

4. Attend the IFSP meeting with the family, Child Find, DECC, and other involved agencies to provide information about Denver Options service providers (DECC will schedule the meeting after consulting with the necessary participants regarding time). This will transpire when there are Denver Options resources to pay for services.

5. Determine with the family the service provider(s) and resources to pay for services.

6. Develop a form for parents to sign if there is a denial of services recommended by Child Find or other professionals.

7. Will provide service coordination for families who receive financial resources from Denver Options.

8. Monitor the service provision and the IFSP.

9. Schedule the six month review and will invite the people that the family would like involved.

10. Offer families the ability to select a service coordinator if the assigned service coordinator proves unsatisfactory.

11. Report changes in supports and services to DECC as they occur (for Part C data collection).

12. Will refer families to DECC for Payor of Last Resort dollars when Denver Options resources are expended and will include a functional outcome relating to the request.

Denver Children and Families Program will:

- Accept referrals from the participating agencies for three levels of support.

- Review referral for potential eligibility for services and supports under Part C.

- Share information and explain to the family the interagency process.

- After receiving family consent, contact DECC to receive the assignment of a service coordinator.
- Complete data count information for those families not giving consent for referral.
- Be involved with the family and the service coordinators at one of three levels of service.

1. **Consultation** (DHCP does not receive a referral)

   - Children that the service coordinator has questions or concerns around health/medical issues. Questions about:
     - Medical Home, have questions about where the child is/should receive health/medical services.
     - Payor source for health services.
     - How the condition of the child might impact the child/family now or in the future (anticipatory guidance).
     - Evaluation choices, considering the condition of the child.
     - Eligibility for HCP paid services.
     - Siblings or other children living in the home.
     - An actual diagnosis.
     - A general sense of feeling that something unknown is going on with a child.

   - Ideally, Consultation will occur before the IFSP process has been initiated. This will allow time for DHCP to make recommendations around the type of evaluation and expected health/medical services.

   - Service coordinator contacts DHCP staff for:
     - Resource/referral information.
     - May elect that we become involved at a monitoring level which would require a referral.

   - Children and Families Staff:
     - Will not be directly involved with the child.
     - Will not participate in the IFSP.
     - Will not be a second signer of the IFSP.

   - Parental consent not required for consultation, as child/family confidentiality is not breached.

- Service coordinator will complete the Part C count and keep it updated (with input from involved agencies).

Some examples of conditions/diagnosis that might fall under this category of DHCP activity level:

- Strabismus
- Isolated Motor Concerns
- Failed Hearing Screen
- CRCSN questions
- Prematurely with no complex health/medical condition
- Child has dysmorphic features
- Delays with no known cause
- Obvious physical anomaly with no known diagnosis

Consultation may yield a referral for Monitoring or Care Coordination.

2. **Monitoring**
   DHCP

   - Referral received by DHCP or generated by the service coordinator.
   - DHCP team will review referral, in order to determine the anticipated level of involvement. May incorporate information from the family, primary provider, or medical record.
   - Level of involvement will be communicated to the service coordinator.
   - Consent from family is required.
   - Has information about the child and family and has some contact with them.
   - Participate in the initial and review IFSP. Prior notice is necessary in order to allow time to obtain and review information about the child's condition.
   - Assess, advocate, and make recommendations around the health/medical and developmental needs.
   - Provide technical assistance to support the implementation of services listed on the IFSP. This does not include being a second signer for the IFSP.
   - DHCP staff will not be listed on the IFSP as

the person responsible for implementation of supports and services. Will provide resource/referral information and be an advocate for health/medical concerns.

- The need for ongoing care coordination needs will be determined during the transition IFSP/IEP process.

- If continuation of services is indicated at the time of transition, DHCP will provide Care Coordination Services.

- This level of involvement may yield a referral for more direct Care Coordination Services.

Service Coordinator

- Provides ongoing follow-up and support that the families are able to access the recommended services.

- Assess with family input that the services are acceptable and related to the functional outcomes.

- Responsible for the administrative aspects of Denver Options funding and Denver Early Childhood Connections payor of last resort funding.

- Will complete the Part C count and keep it updated (with input from involved agencies).

Potential descriptors for this level of involvement:

- Stable, noncomplex health/medical condition.

- Child has a "medical home."

- Premature baby with known health/medical condition or a suspected change in the health/medical condition.

The determination of who will facilitate payor sources (Medicaid, insurance) for natural environments will be negotiated by the involved agencies.

3. Care Coordination Provided
DHCP

- Referral received at DHCP or from service coordinator.

- DHCP team will review referral in order to determine the anticipated level of involvement. May incorporate information from the family, primary provider, or medical record.

- Level of involvement will be communicated to the service coordinator.

- Providing or will provide Care Coordination for the family.

- Actively involved from the time of referral in the planning and decision-making around the process of eligibility determination, type of evaluation, IFSP planning, and IFSP implementation.

- Make recommendations regarding health/medical, developmental needs.

- Provide Care Coordination to facilitate the implementation of health/medical services.

- DHCP staff are listed on the IFSP as the person(s) who will be providing follow-up for concerns or will negotiate responsibilities for the team.

- Responsible for administrative aspects of HCP funding.

Service Coordinator

- Will explain parents' rights and procedural safeguards of Part C under IDEA.

- Will monitor IFSP time frames.

- Will help schedule the IFSP meetings for review and transitions.

- Will complete the Part C count and keep it updated (with input from involved agencies).

- Is responsible for the administrative aspects of Denver Options funding and Denver Early Childhood Connections payor of last resort funding.

Characteristics of children in this category:

- Recommendations for Special Needs Clinic

- Help facilitate the follow-up with Special Needs Clinic

- HCP paid services

- Medically fragile

SIGNATURES OF APPROVAL FOR THIS
INTERAGENCY COMMUNITY PARTNERSHIP AGREEMENT

For: **Denver Early Childhood Connections**

_____   _____
Signature   Date

_____
Title

For: **Denver Public Schools Child Find**

_____   _____
Signature   Date

_____
Title

For: **Denver Options**

_____   _____
Signature   Date

_____
Title

For: **Denver Health Children and Families Program**

_____   _____
Signature   Date

_____
Title

Las Vegas, NV, Greater Metropolitan Clark County CPP Team Profile August 1999–May 2000

1. **Team Description**—The Greater Metropolitan Clark County CPP Team was an interagency task force made up of parents and professionals representing the agencies listed under #2. They met from August 1999 to May 2000 to develop a shared vision and a vehicle of communication that results in the enhancement of early childhood services for children aged birth through eight and their families.

   During participation with the CPP, the team set goals and objectives for service delivery, transition, training, and public awareness issues. The first priority they ended up working on was raising public awareness of community resources for young children and their families.

2. **Partners**—This was a group representing early intervention services, the medical community, family/home daycare, community preschools, Head Start/Early Head Start, community college/university faculty involved in early childhood personnel preparation, Clark County School District, and child/family support systems that essentially functioned as an interagency coordination council. They serve all children birth through eight and their families in metropolitan Clark County, but with particular emphasis upon those children with disabilities or who are at risk in terms of needing special education and/or related services. Partners included:

   - Special Children's Clinic
   - Equal Opportunity Board—CCAD
   - Clark County School District, Preschool
   - Nevada Department of Education, Preschool Special Education Coordinator
   - Oldham Family Learning Center
   - Special Children's Clinic
   - First Step, Division of Child and Family Services
   - Clark County Elementary Schools
   - CCSD, Seigle Center
   - Community Connections/Part C
   - Nellis Child Development Center, Air Force Base
   - Nevada PEP (Parent Training and Information Center)

3. **History and Development**—The state preschool special education coordinator requested assistance from the CPP. New to his position, he wanted to use the project model to increase opportunities for interagency collaboration in Las Vegas. A group of stakeholders received written invitations to attend the first meeting in August 1999 with the following stated purpose:" We will use our knowledge of systems and policies not only to formulate a new vision for young children in Las Vegas, but also to develop meaningful written action plans. We may find that policies need to be changed or modified as we focus on natural environments and the least restrictive environment for all children. Our action plans might include recommendations for policy change at local as well as at the state level. The outcome will be teams of practitioners, parents, and other stakeholders working together with shared goals to create and/or to elevate quality, accessible services and support for young children with special needs and their families."

   The first few meetings were well attended. Discussions were lively and spirited as team members tried to sort out definitions for natural environments, least restrictive environments, and quality services for young children and their families. They did come to consensus that Las Vegas was known more as a playground/vacation area for adults, rather than a community devoted to families and children. Services for young children did exist, but were stretched to the breaking point due to extraordinary population growth in the area (one of the fastest growing communities in the country).

   The team developed a shared vision for service delivery, transition, training, and public awareness issues. After prioritizing community needs in these areas, the team decided to focus on raising public awareness about early intervention resources in the community. They mapped out a target audience, defined a simple message to convey ("Las Vegas families love their children!"), listed public agencies to ask for funding support, and brainstormed different ways that the message could be disseminated through brochures, phone books, etc. University students and possibly the gaming industry could help get the word out. Next steps for all of the above were carefully planned at the November meeting.

At that point, the outside facilitator didn't attend the next few meetings. The group attendance also fell sharply, due to scheduling conflicts, budget cuts, and possibly due to lack of interest in the new priority. A marketing consultant was invited to the February meeting to discuss social marketing concepts, but this meeting was poorly attended and that consultant may have overwhelmed the members of the team that did attend.

The March meeting produced a list of project objectives. The team developed new public awareness activities based on the following community needs:

- Little or no coordinated referral system or information service in place.
- Parents don't know where to call.
- Childcare providers don't know where to send families.
- Phone book is not helpful.
- Lack of awareness of Project Assist Hotline.
- Statistics of prevalence of children with special needs per capita.

In April, a small but mighty team (six people) met at the Nellis Air Force Base Child Development Center to reflect on the project's work to date. They concluded that new partnerships and relationships had been developed but an increasing lack of commitment/attendance by key stakeholders was problematic. The core team then developed short term timelines to finish creating and disseminating a marketing piece to increase public awareness about early intervention resources and to broadcast easy contact information for these resources. The preschool special education coordinator offered to help fund the effort and a couple team members offered to take the

lead in developing the campaign to advertise Child Find. They wanted to finish their year-long commitment to the task force with success!

4. **Results**—Materials with information on how and when to contact Child Find resources were acquired, developed, and disseminated throughout the community over the next few months.

5. **Resources**—Different agencies contributed to the marketing effort with funds or volunteer energy, including the Economic Opportunity Board, Nevada PEP (Parent Training and Information Center), Preschool Special Education discretionary funds, and Nellis AFB Child Development Center.

6. **Sustaining and Replicating (Carrying On After the CPP Facilitator Leaves)**—The team never entirely gelled and had a difficult time after the outside facilitator left. The tremendous rate of population growth in this community continued to put constraints on everyone's time and energy and, eventually, commitment to the project. The original convenor, the state preschool special education coordinator, planned to involve more state level agencies to reach out to the local agencies and provide some motivation and momentum. However, early intervention and early childhood special education needs were not perceived as a priority among the numerous competing interests at the state level.

7. **Lessons Learned in Relation to the CPP Model**—

- *Who's in charge?* This group performed better with an outside, neutral facilitator. Allegiance and commitment to the group were fragile and needed lots of encouragement. The local stakeholders struggled to develop cohesion and were not successful in establishing a unique group identity. The team was still learning to be a team, much less trying to facilitate a struggling group. Different members of the team tried to facilitate but background turf and power issues tended to overshadow and get in the way of progress. A few dedicated members were able to achieve results in spite of the overall diminishing enthusiasm.

- *What's in it for me (or my agency)?* The vision and goals of the planning group need to be perceived as highly important for each member in attendance. Raising public awareness of early intervention resources may not have been crucial enough for all members to continue participation. Local agencies may not have felt enough state agency support for the extra energy that this kind of interagency collaboration takes. While not visible, there are "boundaries" that separate state agency representatives (e.g., preschool special education coordinator) from local program directors, and, as such, they do not operate as equals or colleagues in a functional sense. Thus, state agency representatives may encourage the development of a local vision, but they can not impose their vision upon the locals. Ultimately, state level representatives must find ways to cultivate leadership at the local level so that the vision resulting in systemic change is homegrown.

- *The outside world intervenes!* The rapid population growth in Las Vegas has impacted each agency on the team. There are not enough resources to provide quality services for new families moving to the area. For the past decade these local providers have operated in a survival mode, because an average of 5,000 new people a month have relocated to this area. In this kind of crisis mode and amid constant change, it is very challenging to work on comprehensive systems change. When agency needs are conceptualized in terms of Maslow's Hierarchy (1987) within this environment, systemic change is far up the ladder.

The team responded by narrowing and prioritizing their vision into a manageable task of increasing public awareness. They should feel a measure of success in addressing the realization of their first priority. They can work on the other issues of service delivery, transition, and training in the future, after they create a shared vision regarding what they desire to accomplish. However, it will probably be some time before there is appropriate ecological support such that systemic change is perceived as a priority at both the state and local levels.

8. **Where Are They Now (Winter 2001–02)?** Child Find information produced by Part C was disseminated. The team met immediately after the CPP facilitator left. However, due to turnover in team leadership, the team eventually stopped meeting in spite of an attempt to develop new leadership and get the team going again. Nevertheless, beneficial spin-offs continue. For example, the Special Children's Clinic is beginning to ally with other groups like the Nellis Air Force Base Child Development Center and private preschools. This interagency collaboration has strengthened due to the work begun by CPP. The school district and Head Start have also increased collaboration. This has not been an easy process, but CPP got the ball rolling and it is continuing to roll. Finally, CPP staff/project support for inclusion and natural environments gave validity to Part C efforts in this regard. They were no longer seen as the "radicals" or the messenger with bad news but as part of the national effort for best practices. CPP's push for inclusion gave the Part C people more credibility. Since then, the team has been more open to hearing about inclusion and has brought in national speakers to learn more about providing natural environments and learning opportunities.

South Kingstown, RI, CPP Team Profile January–November 2000

1. **Team Description**—South Kingstown, RI, CPP team was a group of parents and professionals representing the agencies listed under #2 committed to ensuring comprehensive, collaborative, cost effective, culturally competent, quality, inclusive, family friendly services for ALL children prenatal through grade two and their families as it relates to early care and education.

   During CPP participation, the team focused on (a) developing mechanisms to assist families and professionals in accessing community services, (b) blending resources to expand early childhood care and education service options for young children and their families, and (c) coordinating and expanding parenting programs.

2. **Partners**—In order to keep the team workable in size and scope, it was composed of individuals whose agency or interest was directly linked to the current focus of the team. These individuals are referred to as "regular members." The team also involved "contributing/ad hoc members" on an as needed/consultative basis, having them meet with the team periodically related to a relevant issue, seeking their input on key issues via a phone call, having a team member interview them, etc. This team had a core team of approximately 15 members, involving other community stakeholders not only as "contributing/ad hoc members" but also via action teams for each of its priorities that resulted in total team involvement of approximately 45 people.

Regular Members:

- Children's Services, South Shore Mental Health
- Diversity Task Force
- Early Intervention, RI Department of Health
- Early Literacy Program, Hazard and Peace Dale Schools, South Kingstown Schools
- Elementary School Administrator
- Family representatives of children in Early Intervention, Head Start, child care, and public school programs
- First grade teacher, South Kingstown Schools
- Hazard School (Various School Team Members), South Kingstown Schools
- Head Start
- Parents as Teachers of South Kingstown
- SORICO/Child Outreach
- South County Community Action
- South Kingstown School Committee
- South Kingstown Schools, Director of Pupil Personnel
- South Kingstown Schools, Superintendent
- URI Child Development Center
- YMCA of South County

Contributing/Ad Hoc Members:

- A Place to Grow Child Care Center
- Campaign to Eliminate Childhood Poverty
- Cane Child Development Center
- C.A.R.E.S. (Connecting All Resources for Educational Supports)
- Genesis Welfare to Work Program
- Health Center of South County
- South Kingstown Housing Authority
- South Kingstown Library
- South Kingstown Parks and Recreation
- South Kingstown Police Department

3. **History and Development**—Although they had a history of collaborating from agency to agency, they had not collaborated as a communitywide team such as this prior to becoming involved in the CPP. The CPP provided a mechanism to expand these existing collaborations into a formal comprehensive, collaborative communitywide effort. The CPP facilitator worked with this team from January–June 2000 with follow-up phone/e-mail support through Fall 2000 and participation in the team's presentation to the School Committee (Local Board of Education) work session in November 2000. The team began operating on their own in June 2000.

4. Results—When the CPP team started in January 2000, Hazard School (South Kingstown's public school preschool/kindergarten centralized program) was scheduled to close in 2001. That was a major impetus for this team wanting to be a CPP team. While the kindergartens were scheduled to be moved to their home elementaries, plans still needed to be developed regarding the future location of the five inclusive preschool classes, referred to as the South Kingstown Inclusive Preschool (SKIP). There was no Head Start in South Kingstown. A limited number of South Kingstown children attended a Head Start program in a nearby town, but this facility had been deemed inappropriate for continued use. There were 23 South Kingstown children on the Head Start waiting list. The South Kingstown School Committee had many competing priorities in this fast growing and upwardly mobile community. The School Committee wanted longitudinal data on South Kingstown children to demonstrate early childhood efficacy.

The team established a long-term vision related to children ages prenatal through grade two. Within this age range, it established these long term goals: (1) a comprehensive, high quality, inclusive, collaborative birth through age five early childhood service center, (2) a "Direction Service" to assist families and agencies in locating needed services, and (3) a mechanism to coordinate and provide comprehensive parenting programs. To date, accomplishments have included:

a) *Team/School Committee Relations*— The CPP team presented to the School Committee on various occasions on its goals for achieving this vision. These sessions were a means of dialogue between the team and the School Committee resulting in a recognition that the CPP team's goals were consistent with the South Kingstown School Department's strategic plan and the philosophy of school committee members.

b) *Newsletter*—The team planned an Early Childhood Care and Education Newsletter to disseminate strategically in the community to build support for early childhood among key agencies, families, community leaders, civic organizations, the business community, etc. It will contain information on the CPP team and articles about initiatives of the various CPP team members (priority yet to be implemented as of 11/01).

c) *Blended Resources Pilot Program*—The team developed a proposal for an early childhood pilot program using "blended" resources to be located in a public school classroom beginning in 2001–02. They surveyed communities in Kentucky, Colorado, and Illinois regarding use of blended resources. The survey was developed using input from the superintendent regarding issues of concern to him and the School Committee (see survey at the end of the South Kingstown Team Profile). A compilation of this information was used to develop the Pilot Program. The team met with the head of the state's Medicaid agency to discuss how to "blend" education and human services funds. Team members also visited blended programs in Rhode Island and Connecticut. The team submitted this proposal to the School Committee in Winter 2001.

d) *South Kingstown Inclusive Preschool (SKIP)*—The school department decided that these preschool classes would stay at Hazard during 2001–02. This gave preschool classes a definite place to be— and a transition year without the kindergartens—while the CPP team continued to work on the communitywide early childhood center concept, including operation of the Pilot Program.

e) *Head Start Program in South Kingstown*—Head Start found classroom space in South Kingstown with the support of other CPP team members (e.g., public schools, YMCA, etc.). The YMCA offered to provide transportation as this had previously been a major problem for families to be able to access these services. Parent needs at that time did not necessitate accessing this transportation, but it was an option if needed.

f) *Parents As Teacher (PAT) Play Group at the YMCA*—In November 2000, PAT established a playgroup at the YMCA. PAT provided the funding and staff for this program. The YMCA provided the space, play equipment, and some staff support.

g) *Early Childhood Program Efficacy Study*—The South Kingstown School Department engaged a consultant regarding longitudinal data to yield data on previous SKIP graduates and to design a model that could be embedded in early childhood expansions as they move forward. In addition, the CPP team compiled national efficacy data for sharing with the School Committee.

h) *Service Directory*—In order to facilitate "one stop shopping," the team has developed a service directory for parents and agency staff. It was made available in hard copy and will also be available on the South Kingstown School Department's website.

i) *Calendar of Events for Families*—The team compiled a calendar to coordinate existing parenting programs. Compilation was also a tool for identifying service gaps. The calendar was intended to ultimately be available to the public as part of their various strategies to promote community awareness of early childhood.

j) *Early Childhood Center*—One of the team's major long-term goals was a comprehensive, inclusive, collaborative birth–five early childhood service center. This would be a program with services for ALL children ages infancy–five years including children with and without special needs. It would offer direct services to children through a developmentally appropriate early care and education program as well as related supports for families such as comprehensive parenting programs, resource materials, etc. The goal would be to have this center in

place by 2002–03. It was assumed services would continue to be offered in various locations as well as at this center. For example, the center might be the "home" for services that actually delivered in other settings, e.g., early intervention services provided in home, child care, or other natural settings. Also, the center was not intended to displace already existing services nor discourage other service development. Although not fully implemented, much progress toward the vision was made.

In addition to these tangible results, the team identified these benefits and successes:

- Broadening awareness throughout the community, especially by the administration and the School Committee of the importance of early childhood care and education services.

- Connecting school community with other agencies, building bridges in all directions.

- Opening of minds and doors across the community.

- Elimination of duplication of efforts (parallel services) and spending; maximizing impact of dollars available.

- Expansion of service options based on an understanding of what other agencies/organizations offer, e.g., new Child Outreach Screening.

- Involvement of other town services in enthusiastic support of early childhood education, e.g., local libraries.

- Renewal of professional pride by local early childhood care and education professionals.

- Feelings of relief, i.e., "I can focus on what I love to do instead of selling or saving what I do."

- Knowing there is strength in numbers.

- Feelings of hope for the children and families in our community.

- Creativity and synergy.

- Growth.

- The value of mutual respect and support for one another—professional to professional and person to person.
- Shared accomplishments are a positive reflection on all.
- South Kingstown has become a model program!

5. Resources—

- The service directory was printed with resources through the South Rhode Island Educational Collaborative (SORICO).
- The service directory was set up on the South Kingstown School Department website.
- Though not utilized, the YMCA offered to provide transportation for children attending the Head Start program in South Kingstown.
- Parents as Teachers (PAT) established a playgroup at the YMCA. This was a collaboration of resources including PAT funding and staff for the program with the YMCA providing the facility, play equipment, and some staff support.
- Many activities were carried out as part of the regular job roles of various CPP Team members. To this extent, personnel, facility, and operational support (e.g., mailings, office supplies) were provided on an in-kind basis by the team members.

6. Sustaining and Replicating (Carrying On After the CPP Facilitator Leaves)—By June 2000, the team had confirmed the following regarding its operation:

Cochairs: A family representative and a South Kingstown School Department administrator.

Membership: Core team of approximately 15 people with other key stakeholders involved via action plan teams, in "consultant/ad hoc" capacities, etc.

Team Purposes:

1. Oversee coordination, implementation, and evaluation of the team's three action plans.
2. Receive needs assessment resulting from activities associated with action plans. Review this information as available and decide on next steps. Information may include:

- Review of direction service "directory information/database" to ascertain current service capabilities and gaps. Then, review information on types of requests that direction service gets to look for trends related to service needs.
- Review data collected by blended services team on service needs and priorities related to communitywide early care and education needs.
- Review data on current parent training/supports regarding community capabilities and gaps.

3. Facilitate communication/collaboration so that agencies share but do not duplicate resources
4. Develop strategies to keep key stakeholders involved to build support for CPP goals: consumers/beneficiaries, agency heads, potential funders, community leaders, etc.
5. Provide direction in seeking out funding for action plans so CPP team initiatives do not end up competing against each other for resources.

Team Authority: This is not a decision-making/policy setting group; rather, it is a recommending group. It does make decisions on its recommendations, which stem from team consensus. Ultimate decisions are made by the respective entities represented on this group.

7. Lessons Learned in Relation to the CPP Model—The South Kingstown team learned that there is no answer or "simple recipe" to follow that will guarantee effective collaboration. Rather, collaboration is a process that the team has to experience by doing. The CPP model provides a frame for this process, but the team has to actually work through it, learning from the inevitable ups and downs of such a process. And when they do, "many minds make great work!"

• **Shared Leadership Commitment**—This has been essential. By not excluding any key player, it has helped make it clear that early childhood and the efforts of this team are not unique to any one agency, that is, it is not a "school department effort," but rather a true community effort. By joining together, the team now has credibility and a voice through which it is building a broad base of public support. Having a team representative of so many key early childhood interests helped the team determine community needs without guessing. The collective knowledge and resources also led to creativity and synergy.

• **Facilitation**—Starting out with an outside facilitator was helpful, because it helped the team focus on a collective agenda, rather than letting a single agenda dominate. The facilitator helped the team see the bigger picture, sharing information on recommended practice, national trends and models, and what CPP teams in other Rhode Island communities were doing. This helped the team learn from others and "not feel alone," but rather feel empowered as part of a national scene.

The facilitator served as a model for the team, increasing their awareness of the importance of issues such as having an agenda, staying focused and on task in meetings, and having minutes to summarize discussion and decisions and to clearly define next steps. Team participation also resulted in the team learning a variety of facilitation processes. During Action Planning, the team was subdivided into Action Planning teams. The facilitator trained them in how to do Action Planning and gave them handouts with specific instructions and time to practice with the facilitator being there for support. Then, they met separately as Action Planning teams, having a chance to practice their facilitation skills on their own. In this way, the facilitator gave the team "roots and wings."

• **Team Structure for Collaboration**—The team has a core team structure, using action teams (committees) of people, some of whom are on the action team and some of whom are not. At the initial meeting or two,

many agencies were represented. After the team narrowed its focus and began its actual work, there was some level of "fallout" of membership. In retrospect, they realized that this is a natural and evolutionary thing. That is, once the focus is solidified, initial participants can decide whether or not they are willing or able to remain involved. This results in a core team of people who are truly committed and who are able to fully participate in team activities. Those individuals for whom the team has only limited relevance can then be involved as "contributing/ad hoc members" as needed.

• **Stakeholder Involvement**—This team experienced what many teams do, that is, the need to reignite enthusiasm to maintain the team after its initial organization. This was particularly true after summer vacation during which a number of the team members were not working or on vacation, making team meetings difficult to have when everyone could attend. To keep stakeholder involvement high, the team feels it is important to share responsibility for team activities—both so that a few do not get overwhelmed and so that as many people as possible have an opportunity to contribute that is a reason for them to be at the meetings. Stakeholder involvement is a direct link with team accomplishments. That is, the more involvement you have, the better your accomplishments. Likewise, the more you accomplish, the more motivated people are to be involved.

• **Visioning**—The team's vision: "Ensuring comprehensive, collaborative, cost effective, culturally competent, quality, inclusive, family friendly services for ALL children prenatal through grade two and their families as it relates to early care and education. Over the next three to five years, we hope to achieve this vision through establishing a Direction Service and an Early Care and Education Center to build on the foundation of existing community services and, thereby, ensure that ALL children and their families have full and easy access to appropriate early care and education services."

Lessons we have learned about visioning: The vision is an evolutionary thing. It starts out as words on paper. As you make progress toward your vision, it begins to become more real. As you progress, the team should revisit and fine-tune to be more concrete and keep with team members' evolving perspectives. Time spent in developing the vision is very important, because it gives the team a focus. You can't touch lightly on this activity.

- **Priority setting (Thinking Big and Starting Small)**—The team established the following priorities with action teams for each. As of November 2000, some of these priorities were accomplished and some were in progress:

a) Direction Services Action Team
  - "One stop" access point for community resources with universal release of information/confidentiality form to facilitate referrals.
  - Service directory.
  - Website for directory and other information, e.g., parenting programs, public awareness, etc.
  - Public awareness activities and resources, e.g., Fall Festival (linked with Parenting Programs Action Team).

b) Blended Services Action Team
  - Establishment of services to address unmet needs in South Kingstown using "blended" funding and other supports from multiple agencies/sources.
  - Ultimate goal: Model, comprehensive, inclusive early childhood center serving children infancy through kindergarten (not to the exclusion of other services in the South Kingstown "service array").

c) Parenting Programs Action Team
  - Start by coordinating existing parenting programs and supports and making parents aware of these (e.g., a calendar of events, Fall Festival linked with Direction Services Action Team).
  - Establish new parenting programs and supports to address unmet needs.

Lessons learned about priority setting: Breaking things down into short-term goals with manageable steps helps the team develop a sense of accomplishment and motivation to do more. This approach leads to "successive approximation," working incrementally toward attainment of the team vision. They have concluded that if you think big and start small, you'll be amazed at what you can accomplish!

- **Action Planning**—Developing specific action plans helped the group solidify direction and establish a model/structure for team accountability.

- **Implementation of Action Plans**—Having these plans is very important to give concrete and specific direction to whoever needs to do what when, etc. However, completing the plan is only the beginning. Achieving the action plan outcomes necessitates having a variety of strategies in place and adapting those strategies as needed. That is, as the team begins implementing plans, it will learn new things, get new information or resources, get input from each other, etc. This, in turn, will bring about the need to adjust plans and, even, the vision accordingly. Strategies need to attend not only to getting the task done but also to developing positive relationships within and outside of the team. That is, the team should be sensitive to accommodating the workstyles and personalities of team members and the people in the community whose support the team needs.

- **Evaluation of Team Activities**—The team feels that it is very important to formally evaluate its progress at key points, determining both if they accomplished what they set out to do and if those accomplishments have moved them toward their vision. They also feel that it is important for the team to routinely dedicate a small amount of time at its meetings to have a conversation in which they reflect on what they are doing. These reflections help team members develop mutual understandings of what they are experiencing and keep the team on common ground.

8. Where Are They Now (Winter 2001–02)? This team is continuing to meet monthly.

In its November 2001 report to the South Kingstown School Committee, it noted the following accomplishments: (1) Locating Head Start at South Road Elementary School and Hazard School along with the SKIP (South Kingstown Integrated Preschool) has enabled twice as many families to participate in the program. Head Start has doubled the number of children served with the previous obstacles of space and transportation having been overcome. (2) Head Start now runs parent groups at Hazard. (3) Head Start and SKIP children engage in blended activities as a result of the collaboration of educators and co-location of the two programs at Hazard. (4) Collaborative educational playgroups include: (a) Head Start and Early Intervention; (b) Early Intervention coordinated with South Kingstown Parks and Recreation; and (c) Parents As Teachers bi-monthly playgroups at the YMCA, which Early Intervention families attend. (5) CASSP blended a program on children's mental health with the YMCA in summer 2001. (6) Collaboration between the school district and Child Outreach (Child Find) coordinated by the Southern Rhode Island Educational Cooperative (SORICO) is resulting in extensive early screenings: (a) In August 2001, 200 screenings of South Kingstown incoming kindergarteners at Hazard School; (b) screenings at Hazard School of South Kingstown's three- to five-year-olds, including students in the SKIP program; and (c) screening for all South Kingstown Head Start students at Hazard and South Road School. In the past, it was too difficult to complete these screenings due to space and transportation issues. In addition, the Child Outreach Coordinator can now be reached two days a week at Hazard School thereby making Child Outreach Services easily accessible. (7) Parents As Teachers now works with five families at Curtis Corner Elementary. (8) The South Kingstown Housing Authority has expressed an interest in bringing early childhood services to Curtis Corner Road families. (9) The South County YMCA offers childcare for families with kindergarteners, making full day services available. (10) The Visiting Nurses Services (VNS) Family Outreach Program (agency with the earliest access to families of young children) is enthusiastic about collaborating with CPP agencies. (11) CPP is in contact with other key local collaboratives such as the Risk Response Team and the University of Rhode Island's "It Takes a Village." (12) SORICO has updated the CPP Services Directory which supports CPP's first goal "to establish a one stop resource and referral service." (13) The use of Hazard School has allowed participating CPP agencies to model a COZ (Child Opportunity Zone) or community school approach without any new funding. As a result of discussions at the November 2001 School Committee meeting, the CPP team is submitting a budget request to them for continued and expanded use of Hazard School and for an early childhood coordinator position for the 2002–03 budget (this position does not now exist).

Survey of Blended Early Care and Education Services
for Young Children and their Families
June 2000

Survey Explanation: This survey was conducted by two South Kingstown, RI, CPP team members via phone interviews to learn how other communities were "blending" funds from different payors to provide comprehensive early care and education services to young children within the age range of birth through age five. The questions were developed, in part, based on a request for information from the School Committee (board of education) and the superintendent. The questions were crafted during a team session with the superintendent. Sites selected in Kentucky, Colorado, and Illinois for interview were identified by CPP staff. Information obtained from this survey helped the team (1) see concrete examples of other communities achieving blended services much like the South Kingstown vision, (2) acquire information on strategies for blending services and funding sources (e.g., state child care funding, parent fees for child care, preschool special education funds, state education funds for at-risk children, Head Start funds, education funds under Title I, and Even Start), and (3) get practical advice from others "in the trenches." Later the team used questions such as these to guide their visits to programs with blended services in Rhode Island and Connecticut.

Survey Questions:

1. Related to services/program model:

- What types of children are being served, e.g., age range, typical, at risk, children with disabilities, etc.?

- What is your basic program model?

- What services are being provided?

- What is your service schedule e.g., hours of your sessions, times of year you operate, etc.?

2. Related to fiscal issues:

- What resources are being blended and how are these being used? That is, does money change hands and if so, how? Or, are other blending options used? E.g., does one agency provide a building, another transportation, others particular services, another food services, etc.?

- What is the cost per child for the various service options you provide? E.g., center-based vs. home-based vs. full day vs. half day, etc.?

- What accounting considerations are necessary for such blending?

- Do you charge any parent fees? If not, why not? If so, what fees are charged and for what?

3. Related to start-up:

- How did you come to provide a blended program? What was the impetus?

- What factors were key to your success? What advice would you give others who are attempting to set up a blended program? What would you suggest that they do? What pitfalls should they try to avoid?

4. *Related to buy-in:*

- How did you get the buy-in of the agency heads/officials and governing boards of the various agencies whose resources are being blended? At the state level? At the local level?

- Who were your local level key decision-makers from the participating agencies? Please provide name, agency, and contact information if available.

- How did you get the buy-in of the staff of the various agencies whose resources are being blended?

- How did you get the buy-in of the parents of the various agencies whose resources are being blended?

- How did you/do you build community buy-in/support for early childhood services?

5. *Related to efficacy/program evaluation:*

- Do you have any data on how these children and their families are impacted by your services—both short-term and long-term?

6. *Related to materials on your program that we might share with our team:*

- Do you have brochures or any other public awareness materials you could share with us?

Longmont, CO, St. Vrain Early Childhood Council CPP Team Profile 2000–2001

1. **Team Description**—The St. Vrain Early Childhood CPP was a group of people representing most of the early childhood service providers in Longmont, CO and the surrounding St. Vrain valley. This geographical region is in between two large catchment areas for school districts and developmental disability services— Boulder and Weld County. The past few years had brought tremendous population growth to this region and participants felt it was time to forge their own identity and plan for comprehensive early childhood systems. They committed to work together to examine, create, and implement optimal early childhood care, support, and education for children (birth through five) and their families in the St. Vrain community.

During CPP participation, the team focused on developing a collaborative system to ensure (1) the availability and accessibility for early identification of children with special needs or who are at risk for future developmental concerns and (2) family supports.

2. **Partners**—Members of the St. Vrain team included representatives from the following local agencies:

- St. Vrain Public Schools Special Education
- Mental health
- Head Start
- Tiny Tim Center
- Public health
- O.U.R. Childcare Center
- Boulder County Early Childhood Connections
- Dayspring Developmental Center
- Boulder Developmental Disabilities Center
- Weld County Family Connects
- Rocky Mountain Preschool
- Bright Beginnings
- Children's Family Services

3. **History and Development**—The CPP project staff originally asked the Colorado Department of Education to recommend a community of early childhood systems that might be poised to begin a year's work as an outreach site working collaboratively on strategic planning. They recommended the town of Longmont and, specifically, the new director of special education for St. Vrain Public Schools. In her role as director, this woman wanted to create an interagency group to guide early childhood systems in the community. The community had grown tremendously and there were key personnel changes in the school district that fostered a lot of enthusiasm for starting a new project. One member wrote in her letter of invitation, "I would like to build upon the existing relationships and collaboration efforts within our early childhood community. The goal of this meeting is to begin to strengthen coordinated systems of early childhood services, improve communication among our agencies, and blend resources so that our limited resources can go farther." People in Longmont were eager to work together and focus on their own community, instead of always being a smaller part of larger county groups with different agendas.

The group began with a full day meeting, in which they began to share their dreams and concerns for young children with special needs in St. Vrain. Additional key stakeholders were identified and invited to future meetings. Parents of young children with special needs were especially encouraged to attend. The first draft vision was developed after two meetings. It reflected the group's high commitment, enthusiasm, and passion for their work but seemed unrealistic for one year or even three years of collaborative work. The team decided to focus primarily on the third section of the vision:

> "To develop a collaborative system to ensure the availability and accessibility for early identification, family supports, and best practice."

The group committed to working together throughout the school year as a collaborative planning team to develop written action plans and an infrastructure for implementation and evaluation. After reading *DEC Recommended Practices* (available from Sopris West), the team realized a key point. They were amazed at how often "family" was mentioned throughout the practices. The planning team had also spent time at each meeting discussing different ways to get more family input into the process and were feeling frustrated in their efforts. They needed to hear from diverse families about their experiences in order to improve quality. There were always a couple of parents of older students with special needs at each meeting—but they wanted to hear current experiences of families interacting at each meeting. Feedback from parents who had been part of state Part C monitoring events and results of the Child Find Evaluation will be used as a beginning step towards more family input into the planning process.

The team then decided to weave ideas from the *Recommended Practices* into their work on the newly prioritized goals that appear in the following boxes.

> **GOAL I:**
> Develop a collaborative system to ensure the availability and accessibility for early identification of children with special needs or who are at risk for future developmental concerns.

> **GOAL II:**
> Develop a collaborative system for family supports.

One of the team members synthesized their work when suggesting the following metaphor: "The community of early childhood systems in St. Vrain is like an old house that has been remodeled and revamped continuously over the years until it has too many rooms. It's hard for a family to find their way from one room to another. We need to take out some of the walls and open it up and make it easy to negotiate. We need to focus on quality as well as practicality as we remodel once again."

4. Results—

a) **Resource Matrix**—The team developed a matrix of all early childhood resources in the St. Vrain region with names and contact information of almost seventy different resources available to support young children and families in Longmont.

The purpose of this matrix was to help the team analyze gaps in resources and identify community needs. The team is considering developing a different version for agencies to give to families.

Agency Names and Contact Info	Screenings and Evaluations	Health Care	Parenting Classes	Special Needs Transpor- tation	Specialized Child Care and/or Education	Mental Health	Financial and/or Emergency Assistance	Support Groups— Advocacy

b) **Child Identification Matrix and Activities Flowchart**—A matrix that listed down one side the names of agencies and then across the top of the matrix in columns whether they provided:

Agencies	General Screen	Vision Screen	Hearing Screen	Developmental Evaluation

This list was the first step in what evolved into a communitywide flowchart for child identification activities.

c) **Assisted in Revising State PR Brochures**— While reviewing different marketing materials from early childhood communities, the team checked the contact phone number listed on a state brochure. It was disconnected. Because many groups across the state had just purchased many of these brochures, a member of the team called the state department and worked with them to develop a sticker to list the correct contact phone number.

d) **Early Childhood Interagency Council**—The St. Vrain Early Childhood Collaborative Planning Project team evolved into a formal interagency council over the course of the school year. This council will provide input to the director of special education regarding comprehensive early childhood systems.

5. **Resources**—The St. Vrain Public School system provided monthly meeting space and mailed minutes of each meeting to all team members. Other agencies provided "in kind" staff time for the monthly meetings.

6. **Sustaining and Replicating (Carrying On After the CPP Facilitator Leaves)**—The CPP facilitator was asked to facilitate the majority of meetings for the first year. At the close of the school year, participants were enthusiastic about continuing on as an interagency council instead of being only a temporary project. They found value and meaning in attending the collaborative planning meetings. The original convenor of the team, the director of special education, was especially pleased with the hard work and diligence that team members put forth during the year and

was eager to continue supporting the council. The school district hired a facilitator to conduct meetings the following year (school year 2001–02).

7. Lessons Learned in Relation to the CPP Model—

- *Stakeholder Energy Levels—*This team was made up of very dynamic and dedicated people. They were skilled administrators, clinicians, teachers, and advocates for young children and families. They dreamed big dreams while creating their original vision. Their overarching premise was inspiring and overwhelming at the same time: "In three years we want to see enough staff to support the early childhood needs of all young children and their families (ages birth through five) in the St. Vrain community and sufficient bilingual professionals to meet the needs of mono-lingual preschool community members provided by early childhood agencies." Based upon this vision, the team listed twenty different goals. When the time came to write specific strategies for each of the goals, the team realized the reality of available time and energy and reprioritized accordingly.

- *The Role of an Interagency Council—*"Goal I: Develop a collaborative system to ensure the availability and accessibility to early identification" is very similar to the goal of Child Find in the public schools. The team tried be very careful not to replicate what the Child Find coordinator was busy doing, but to enhance her efforts by adding coordinated community support through the interagency planning process. The team looked at and continues to look at different ways they can make the whole process easier for young children and their families.

8. Where Are They Now (Winter 2001–02)? The St. Vrain Early Childhood Council continues. They have hired a facilitator with school district funding, because all team members want to be full participants instead of taking turns as facilitator. The district continues to be enthusiastic about the work of the council and will keep this in place in the district for the foreseeable future. Over the past year, the council has produced these results: (1) Resource phone matrix; (2) Single point of entry; (3) Single intake form; (4) Universal consent form; (5) Child Find flowchart; (6) Interagency organizational flowchart; (7) Three county interagency agreements for child identification; (8) Greater understanding of what each agency provides; (9) "Warm Welcome" packet updated (given to all new parents); and (10) Transition written agreement. In addition, member agencies are collaborating on services. Mental health and Child Find have worked collaboratively to serve a group of young children needing supports from schools and from mental health who had not been served previously (those at risk due to emotional and sensory issues). Part C weekly screenings were evaluated by parents and found to be too chaotic and held in a very small, cramped space. Through collaboration with the Developmental Disabilities service agency, the screenings are now held in a very private and quiet space and families are more satisfied.

Westerly, RI, CPP Team Profile September 1999–November 2000

1. Team Description—The Westerly, RI, CPP Team was a group of parents and professionals representing the agencies listed under #2 and committed to increasing the involvement of parents and the community at large in the education and care of their children ages birth to six with and without disabilities with emphasis related to the needs of unidentified, unserved, and underserved children who have developmental delays and behavioral challenges.

During CPP participation, the team focused on:

(a) strengthening linkages with physicians to facilitate early identification and referral of children with special needs and (b) providing training and other supports to increase the awareness of families regarding typical and atypical development, including how they can support their child's development, and regarding accessing services in the community.

2. Partners—In order to keep the team workable in size and scope, it was composed of individuals whose agency or interest was directly linked to the current focus of the team. These individuals were referred to as "regular members." The team also involved "contributing/ad hoc members" on an as-needed/consultative basis, having them meet with the team periodically related to a relevant issue, seeking their input on key issues via a phone call, having a team member interview them, etc.

Regular Team Members:

- Family representatives of children in Early Intervention, Head Start, child care, and public school programs
- Parent Partnership Program of the Westerly School Department
- Parents as Teachers Program, Family Life Education, South Shore Mental Health
- South County Head Start
- South County Community Action Adolescent Self-Sufficiency Collaborative
- Southern Region Early Intervention
- Westerly School Department: (1) Child Outreach and (2) preschool teacher
- YMCA nursery school

Contributing/Ad Hoc Members:

- Rhode Island Department of Health, Division of Family Health
- Westerly School Department, Special Education Director
- Woman's Health Center, Westerly Hospital

3. History and Development—Although they had a history of collaborating from agency to agency, they had not collaborated as a communitywide team prior to becoming involved in the CPP. The CPP provided a mechanism to expand these existing collaborations into a formal comprehensive, collaborative communitywide effort. The CPP facilitator worked with this team from September 1999–March 2000 after which they began operating on their own.

4. Results—As of October 2000, CPP team accomplishments are:

a) *Developmental wheel for communitywide dissemination (particularly targeted at families)*—In order to provide something easy for parents to read related to developmental milestones birth–five, the team purchased a developmental wheel with developmental milestones birth–five that included tips for parents related to important parenting issues such as child development and immunizations. They disseminated this wheel to families via multiples options, e.g., through CPP team member agencies, the public library, physicians' offices, in gift bags, etc.

b) *"Prescription pad" referral form for physicians*—This was completed in spring 2000 and is now in use. Westerly High School did the printing of these prescription pads. The team has provided envelopes for physicians (or families) to return these to either the Child Outreach Office at the schools or to Early Intervention—which will in turn direct the referrals elsewhere if needed. Team representatives met with 15 local physicians, including pediatricians, at the beginning of the 2000–01 school year. They were very receptive about the use of these pads and expressed a desire to get relevant feedback related to their patients. At their suggestion, the Westerly School Department also established a fax line dedicated to Child Outreach referrals in light of confidentiality considerations. (A copy of the "Prescription pad" referral form appears at the end of this profile.)

c) *Outreach to physicians*—The team met with 15 local physicians in August to heighten their awareness of the existence of early childhood resources in this community and the desire of this team to work in greater collaboration with physicians. They intend to continue to communicate with them on a periodic basis for information sharing purposes. In addition, in fall 2000, CPP team members (the South County Community Action Adolescent Self-Sufficiency Collaborative and the Parents as Teachers Program) collaborated with Wood River Health Services on a five-session parenting series.

d) *Family awareness workshops regarding typical/atypical child development*—The team has (a) spoken on the radio about high quality care and (b) conducted training on "Positive Discipline: Building on Strengths" for parents at a community nursery school and at the YMCA (which provides childcare during these sessions). These trainings were a series of four sessions. They were conducted in spring 2000 and repeated during 2000-01. They provided an ongoing story hour for families of young children under the age of three. The team started this story hour in spring 2000, holding it at the board of education. During the 2000-2001 school year (November-February), these were held at the Westerly Parent-Teacher Resource Center with 28 families participating.

e) *Parents as Teachers*—CPP team members developed a Parents as Teachers (PAT) grant—which they received as of June 2000. This program was operated in collaboration with personnel who operated the PAT program through Children's Services, South Shore Mental Health. The new grant was located at the Parent Partnership Program of the Westerly School Department. There were 20 participants in this program—parents of children prenatal–age three. They had bimonthly play groups and offered evening workshops that included a baby-sitting service. They offered special supports for teen parents in collaboration with the South County Community Action Adolescent Self-Sufficiency Collaborative. The CPP team served as the Community Council for the PAT Project, using CPP meetings to review PAT progress and to help with program planning implementation. Some EI and Head Start staff were also trained in the PAT model.

f) *Gift bags*—These were made available to families of newborns and included the developmental wheel, information on resources, toys, coupons, etc. Items included donations from local merchants.

g) *Even Start Grant*—The Westerly School Department received an Even Start Grant. The grant provided resources to support some of the above activities as well as related goals of the Westerly, RI, CPP Team for which action was not originally initiated due to resource limitations. These included activities such as increasing the number of PAT slots, paying for developmental wheels for families, providing transportation for families to attend meetings and appointments, collaborating with the Washington County Adult Learning Program, and providing parent outreach services. The team used a "cluster approach" to services through which Even Start services were provided in existing community partners: (a) Head Start, (b) the public library English as a Second Language (ESL) program, (c) Early Intervention Program, using its building for a program for parents of children ages birth–three with the potential for having an inclusive program there, and (d) YMCA.

In addition to these tangible results, the team identified these accomplishments:

- We have a common commitment to make sure kids needing services are identified at an early age and linked to the resources they need.

- Collaboration has made us aware of new opportunities and broadened our perspective about services in this community. Depending on the situation, these opportunities have sometimes involved just some of the CPP agencies and sometimes all. These collaborations have expanded the capacity of the involved agencies to more fully and effectively meet the needs of children and families.

- We have a sense of accomplishment, because we can see tangible results and products.

- The team provides a vehicle for us to support each other.

- Some communities meet and never do anything. This one does!

- We no longer see kids as belonging to any one agency. These are "Westerly's kids."

5. Resources—

- *Westerly High School*—At a nominal cost, high school students printed the "Prescription pad" referral form for physicians. High school students have also volunteered to stuff gift bags.

- *Parent As Teachers Grant*—This annual grant covered the 2000–01 school year. It could be renewed but, ultimately, would need to be funded through alternative funding sources. Current funding came from the Department of Children, Youth and Families through the Rhode Island Children's Trust. South Shore Mental Health served as the grantee.

- *Even Start Grant*—This annual grant covered the 2000–01 school year. Funding came from the Rhode Island Department of Education. The Westerly School Department served as the grantee.

- Many activities were carried out as part of the regular job roles of various CPP Team members. To this extent, personnel, facility, and operational support (e.g., mailings, office supplies) were provided on an in-kind basis by the team members.

- They continue to pursue various funding options for their activities, e.g., foundation grants, funding from local banks and businesses, etc.

6. Sustaining and Replicating (Carrying On After the CPP Facilitator Leaves)—At the last meeting at which the CPP team facilitator was present, the team identified:

- Three people to share the role of team convenor/facilitator.

- One person to serve as team recorder.

- A schedule to meet every four to six weeks, on Thursdays, 12:30–3:30.

7. Lessons Learned in Relation to the CPP Model—

- *Shared Leadership Commitment*—It is important to get all key players on board at the start. The core of our original team has stayed very committed. As we grew in size, we have had more stakeholders become committed to our team, because they were motivated to join us in the progress we were making. Our commitment is high, in part, because our respective goals overlap to form a common bond.

- *Facilitation*—Having an outside neutral facilitator is very helpful in getting the ball rolling. This was key. That is, we have always had good ideas, but we were slow getting started and following through. Having a facilitator who had the job of helping us get started helped us do so by keeping our focus on our goals and objectives. We learned that it is important to have a team facilitator who is organized and who can help the team move forward with action plans. We learned a step-by-step style of facilitation, using a wonderful model with visual recaps, planning strategies, etc. Then, by the time the facilitator left, team members were able to facilitate, drawing on facilitation skills team members learned together as part of the process. These skills are necessary for continued growth, because we all need to feel that our time is efficiently utilized by the team.

- *Team Structure for Collaboration*—The dedication of our team members to reaching a common goal was exciting to watch. We established a common commitment and goals and stay solution-oriented. It has been wonderful watching this sense of togetherness evolve. What an exciting way to work and reach a goal. As with many committees, there are some who take very active roles and others who take more passive roles. This team has been particularly good at accepting each other's personality, willingness/ability to get things done, etc. The team has operated very harmoniously as a result. If some team members are more visible or more active on one particular priority or another, no one cares, because we all share what is gained by the process.

  Working together as a team promoted creativity and synergy. Everyone has contributed based on their respective strengths. A key to our success was everyone pitching in and volunteering to take an active role. We established a standard procedure of team members reporting on follow-through since the last meeting and other relevant updates at the beginning of each meeting.

Within our core team, we established "action plan teams" or "subteams" so we could "divide and conquer" our priorities and accomplish more, e.g., two people work on prescription pads, two work on developing funding sources, etc.

- *Stakeholder Involvement*—It has been helpful to have a core team dealing with day-to-day issues around the CPP vision and, then, other stakeholders to call upon for specific assistance. Core team members truly have a "stake" in team efforts. That is, all stakeholders who attend regularly appear to get something for their families and give something to the team.

- *Visioning*—The team's vision: "Appropriate supports in our community make it possible for parents of children ages birth to six with typical and atypical development (1) to know about typical and atypical child development and developmentally appropriate practice in order to work with their children and to recognize quality programs and (2) to know what help is available and how to access it."

Learnings about visioning aregarding When you come together as a team committed to a common goal, how easy each step along the way can be! We have realized that achieving our vision is an ongoing process.

- *Priority Setting (Thinking Big and Starting Small)*—The team identified seven major objectives that they hoped would lead to putting this vision in place. They projected staggering implementation of these objectives over a multiyear time frame.

Learnings about priority setting are: Thinking big and starting small is so important. We 100% agree with the importance of starting small. Taking "baby steps" toward our vision worked well, because in these days of change, small manageable goals work best. This is part of the reason the team is still so excited about collaboration, because we've seen things implemented—

some even sooner that expected. Although there is still much to do, we have accomplished a lot!

- *Action Planning*—Our action plans specified who would do what when, etc. This was an effective process that will be ongoing with our team as we address new priorities.

- *Implementation*—We used our plans to guide our work. Implementation includes some trial and error. Team members feel positive about continued implementation, because of what they have accomplished and the teamwork and commitment that has resulted. Seeing things followed through and implemented boosted enthusiasm, helping us see that we can do this and accomplish even bigger goals!

- *Evaluation*—It is important to periodically evaluate progress, seeing what is working and what needs to be changed related to working toward your goals. Only in this way will the team know if it is on track toward its vision.

8. **Where Are They Now (Winter 2001–02)?** All of the original goals have been met or are being worked on, and they have created more. They continue to collaborate on interagency workshops for parents on behavioral issues (childcare provided), the physician's "Prescription pad" referral form, story hour for birth–three-year-olds, and several collaborative grants (Parents As Teachers and Even Start). The physician's "Prescription pad" referral form is so well received that physicians that serve other communities are asking early childhood staff in those communities to use them. Families are approaching Early Intervention and the schools saying that their doctors told them about services. Some physicians have even attended IEP meetings. CPP team members collaborated on an early childhood display at a school district community fair in March 2001. At this fair, they provided gift bags and information for families on early childhood services. In addition to the Even Start program components noted above, this grant has made it possible for the schools to offer wraparound services and meet with families on Saturdays for field trips that are intensive parenting mentorship opportunities.

Team members are also working together on a community basis pursuing National Association for the Education of Young Children (NAEYC) accreditation for school, Head Start, and child care programs (several are now accredited).

Westerly, RI, Collaborative Planning Project Team "Prescription Pad" Physician Referral Form

Physicians are using this form to make referrals to either the Early Intervention Program or the Westerly Public School Department Child

Outreach. Referrals are transmitted either by fax or by return envelopes that were supplied by the Collaborative Planning Team. Collaborative Planning Team members provided these "Prescription pads" to physicians via attending one of the physician's regular meetings at the Westerly Hospital. This referral pad has been so well received that physicians that serve other communities are asking early childhood staff in those communities to use them. Families are approaching Early Intervention and the schools saying that their doctors told them about services. Some physicians have even attended IEP meetings.

REFERRAL

(Birth to five Years)
Early Intervention Program/Westerly Public School Department

NAME: _____ DOB: _____

PARENTS: _____

ADDRESS: _____

TELEPHONE: _____

AREA(S) OF CONCERN: Check Comment

Speech/Language _____ _____

Gross Motor _____ _____

Fine Motor _____ _____

Social/Behavioral _____ _____

Other _____ _____

Doctor's Signature _____ Date: _____

Bibliography

Bryson, J. M. (1988). *Strategic planning for public and nonprofit organizations: A guide to strengthening and sustaining organizational achievement.* San Francisco: Jossey-Bass Publishing.

Daniels, W. (1986). *Group power I: A manager's guide to using task-force meetings.* San Diego: Pfeiffer and Company.

Fay, P. P. & Doyle, A. G. (1982). Stages of group development. In J. E. Jones and J. W. Pfeiffer (Eds.). *The 1982 annual for facilitators, trainers and consultants.* San Diego, CA: University Associates.

Fisher, R., & Ury, W. (1981). *Getting to yes: Negotiating agreement without giving in.* Boston: Houghton Mifflin.

Fullan, M. G. (1993). *Change forces.* New York: The Falmer Press.

Fullan, M. G. (1991). *The new meaning of educational change.* New York: Teachers College Press.

Guskey, T., & Huberman, M. (1995). *Professional development in education: new paradigms and practice.* New York: Teachers College Press.

Hall, G. E., Wallace, R. C., & Dossett, W. E. (1973). *A developmental conceptualization of the adoption process within educational institutions.* Austin: The Research and Development Center for Teacher Education, the University of Texas at Austin.

Hayden, P., Frederick, L., Smith, B. J., & Broudy, A. (2001a). *Developmental facilitation: Helping teams promote systems change.* Denver: Collaborative Planning Project for Planning Comprehensive Early Childhood Systems at the University of CO at Denver. ERIC #ED455628.

Hayden, P., Frederick, L., Smith, B. J., & Broudy, A. (2001b). *Tasks, tips, and tools for promoting collaborative community teams.* Denver: Collaborative Planning Project for Planning Comprehensive Early Childhood Systems at the University of CO at Denver. ERIC #ED455627.

Hayden, P., Smith, B. J., Rapport, M. J., & Frederick, L. (1999). *Facilitating change in comprehensive early childhood systems.* Denver: Collaborative Planning Project for Planning Comprehensive Early Childhood Systems at the University of CO at Denver. ERIC #ED435152.

Maslow, A. (1987). *Motivation and Personality*, 3rd Ed. New York: Harper & Row.

Mintzberg, H. (1994). *The rise and fall of strategic planning.* New York: The Free Press.

Pfeiffer, W. J., Goodstein, L. D., & Nolan, T. M. (1989). *Shaping strategic planning.* Glenview, IL: Scott, Foresman and Company.

Rous, B., Hemmeter, M. L., & Schuster, J. (1999). Evaluating the impact of the STEPS model on development of community-wide transition systems. *Journal of Early Intervention, 22,* 38–50.

Sandall, S., McLean, M. E., & Smith, B. J. (2000). *DEC Recommended Practices in Early Intervention/Early Childhood Special Education.* Longmont, CO: Sopris West.

Schwarz, R. M. (1994). *The skilled facilitator: Practical wisdom for developing effective groups.* San Francisco: Jossey-Bass Publishing.

Senge, P. M. (1990). *The fifth discipline: The art and practice of the learning organization.* New York: Doubleday.

Sparks, D. (1994). A paradigm shift in staff development. *Journal of Staff Development, 15*(4), 26–29.

Smith, B. J., & Rapport, M. J. (1999a). *Early childhood inclusion policy and systems: What do we know?* Denver: Collaborative Planning Project for Planning Comprehensive Early Childhood Systems at the University of CO at Denver. ERIC #ED436035.

Smith, B. J., & Rapport, M. J. (1999b). *IDEA and Early Childhood Inclusion.* Denver: Collaborative Planning Project for Planning Comprehensive Early Childhood Systems at the University of CO at Denver. ERIC #ED436036.

Smith, B. J., & Rose, D. F. (1993). *Administrators policy handbook for preschool mainstreaming.* Cambridge, MA: Brookline Books.

Other helpful references

Ambrose, D. (1987). *Managing complex change.* Pittsburgh, PA: Enterprise Group.

Barth, R. S. (1991). *Improving schools from within.* San Francisco: Jossey-Bass Publishing.

Covey, S. (1989). *The seven habits of highly effective people.* New York: Simon and Schuster, Inc.

Daniels, W. (1990). *Group power II: A manager's guide to using regular meetings.* San Diego: Pfeiffer and Company.

Doyle, M., & Straus, D. (1982). *How to make meetings work.* New York: Berkley Publishing Group.

Fisher, R., & Brown, S. (1988). *Getting together: Building relationships as we negotiate.* New York: Penguin Books.

Kanter, R. M. (1984). *Managing change—The human dimension.* Cambridge, MA: Goodmeasure, Inc.

Owens, R. G. (1987). *Organizational behavior in education.* Englewood Cliffs, NJ: Prentice-Hall, Inc.

Reck, R. R., & Long, B. G. (1987). *The win-win negotiator: How to negotiate favorable agreements that last.* New York: Simon and Schuster, Inc.

Scearce, C. (1992). *100 Ways to Build Teams.* Palatine, IL: IRI/Skyline Publishing.

Schwarz, R. M. (1994). *The skilled facilitator: Practical wisdom for developing effective groups.* San Francisco: Jossey-Bass Publishing.

Senge, P. M., Roberts, C., Ross, R. B., Smith, B. J., & Kleiner, A. (1994). *The fifth discipline fieldbook: Strategies and tools for building a learning organization.* New York: Doubleday.

Ury, W. (1993). *Getting past no: Negotiating your way from confrontation to cooperation.* New York: Bantam Books.